THE

PROTRACTED

GAME

A Wei-ch'i Interpretation

of Maoist Revolutionary Strategy

THE
PROTRACTED
GAME

A Wei-ch'i Interpretation

of Maoist Revolutionary Strategy

SCOTT A. BOORMAN

OXFORD UNIVERSITY PRESS
LONDON   OXFORD   NEW YORK

OXFORD UNIVERSITY PRESS
Oxford   London   New York
Glasgow   Toronto   Melbourne   Wellington
Cape Town   Salisbury   Ibadan   Nairobi   Lusaka   Addis Ababa
Bombay   Calcutta   Madras   Karachi   Lahore   Dacca
Kuala Lumpur   Hong Kong   Tokyo

ACKNOWLEDGMENTS

For their interest and encouragement during the protracted evolution of the thesis presented here, I wish to thank my parents Margaret Echlin Boorman and Howard L. Boorman and my sometime wei-ch'i-opponent Christopher Wright. I am also grateful to Robert W. Adamson for his confidence and to Kensaku Segoe, Kaku Takagawa, and Edward Lasker for their kind response to my request to make use of certain diagrams from their works.

CONTENTS

TABLES

MAPS

MAPS BY VAUGHN GRAY

THE CHINA BOARD
(Provincial boundaries as of 1937)

MAP I

0   500 Miles

THE

PROTRACTED

GAME

A Wei-ch'i Interpretation
of Maoist Revolutionary Strategy

INTRODUCTION

The value and the validity of analysis of a military strategy employed at a given place and time are in great part determined by the strategic preconceptions of the analyst, by his criteria for assessing the importance and the correctness of a given strategic decision. For the Western historian, the degree of which strategic preconceptions hinder interpretive analysis of Western military history is, of course, minimal: the historian is dealing with a portion of his own cultural and intellectual heritage. A similar observation is true of the attitudes and actions of a Western soldier or statesman dealing with an essentially Western conflict situation.[1] The applicability of Western analytic criteria vanishes, however, when the Western analyst, lay or governmental, attempts to confront the strategic techniques of a culture different from his own.[2]

3

Invalidation of the Western strategic framework—or, more precisely, Western strategic values—tends to confuse and distort understanding of non-Western strategic patterns by Western scholars, soldiers, and diplomats. The conscious superiority of an American military officer who, describing the Japanese defense of Guadalcanal, remarked that

> . . . their idea of winning battles was to achieve surprise if possible, otherwise to overwhelm by sheer weight of numbers and indifference to losses. These means failing . . . they abandoned tactics for trickery.[3]

is reflected even more tersely in the words of a former commander of American forces in Vietnam: ". . . we're smarter [than the Vietnamese Communists] . . . and we've got more guts." [4]

Analysis of the Chinese strategic tradition affords no exception to these general propositions. One of the most recent manifestations of this tradition is the Maoist system of revolution applied in China between 1927 and 1949 and in process of application in Southeast Asia since 1946.[5] Fused from both Chinese and Marxist-Leninist elements but strongly Chinese in underlying dynamics, this strategy abounds in paradoxes when judged by the standards of conventional Western military doctrine: its use of fluid operational methods and yet its reliance upon relatively stable base areas; its emphasis on efficiency and yet its tolerance of protraction; and its delight in complexity in contrast to the simplicity of Western warfare. Moreover, Western analysts frequently have difficulty in determining which of the mass of (often propaganda-submerged) principles and patterns found in Chinese Communist-type strategy are most pivotal in the actual implementation of revolution. In short, critical Western analysis of Maoist revolution is severely handi-

4

capped by lack of a systematic framework, or point of view, by which to evaluate and structure the theory and practice of that revolutionary formula.

One tool for resolving the paradoxes and related obstacles that confound the Westerner, or at least for aiding in better understanding of them, would be a simplified form of conflict which could serve to represent accurately the general contours of the classic Maoist revolutionary situation and of the strategy of revolution arising from it, but which did not have the complexity and uncertainty of historical reality. To use, in an informal sense, a term current in political science, we are suggesting the relevance of a simulation model of the processes of Chinese Communist-type revolution.[6] The purpose of evolving a model of this sort, a microcosm which can be used to reflect the essential patterns of the strategy under consideration, is to bridge the gap between the cognitive processes of the Western student of Asian politics on the one hand and those of the Asian revolutionary leader on the other.

A mechanism for avoiding certain difficulties inherent in cross-cultural strategic analysis may be found in the ancient Chinese game of strategy wei-ch'i.[7] Although commonly known in the West under its Japanese name go, and extensively studied in Japan, wei-ch'i has been a favorite game of strategy of Chinese generals, statesmen, and literati from the former Han dynasty (206 B.C.–8 A.D.) to the times of Mao Tse-tung.[8] It is safe to assume that, historically, there has probably been considerable interaction between the strategy of wei-ch'i and the strategy used in Chinese warfare. If indeed wei-ch'i and Chinese Communist strategy are products of the same strategic tradition, wei-ch'i may be more realistically used as an analogic model of that strategy than any purely theoretical structure generated by a Western social scientist. An additional advantage of the use of wei-ch'i is that the game, strategically complex, is better understood as a result of centuries of intensive study by Chinese and Japanese players than could be an equally sophisticated artificial model. But although wei-ch'i was not evolved as a model of Chinese Communist revolutionary strategy, the game's basic processes of play and of command decision may easily be set in correspondence with those of revolutionary, especially military, conflict. The structure of the game, and in particular its abstractness, makes possible a depth of analogy which has no parallel in the relatively superficial comparisons of Western forms of military strategy to chess or poker.

A more direct and positive factor contributing to the potential value of wei-ch'i as a strategic decision model of Chinese Communist insurgent strategy is to be found in the presence of significant comparisons between the strategy of the game and that of revolution in the writings of Mao Tse-tung. In May 1938, in his important essay "Problems of Strategy in Guerrilla War Against Japan," Mao wrote:

> Thus there are two forms of encirclement by the enemy forces and two forms of encirclement by our own—rather like a game of *weichi*. Campaigns and battles fought by the two sides resemble the capturing of each other's pieces, and the establishment of strongholds by the enemy and of guerrilla base areas by us resembles moves to dominate spaces on the board. It is in the matter of "dominating the spaces" that the great strategic role of guerrilla base areas in the rear of the enemy is revealed.[9]

In another essay dating from the same period in the development of Mao Tse-tung's strategic thought, "On Protracted War," he developed these propositions, saying,

> —rather like a game of *weichi*. Campaigns and battles fought by the two sides resemble the capturing of each

6

other's pieces, and the establishment of enemy strongholds (such as Taiyuan) and our guerrilla base areas (such as the Wutai Mountains) resembles moves to dominate spaces on the board. If the game of *weichi* is extended to include the world, there is yet a third form of encirclement as between us and the enemy. . .[10]

Ten years after the publication of "On Protracted War," Mao once again used terminology reminiscent of wei-ch'i. In his campaign directive regarding final operations against the Nationalists in the north China theater in late 1948, entitled in his *Selected Military Writings* "The Concept of Operations for the Peiping-Tientsin Campaign," Mao said, "If these two points, Tangku (the most important) and Hsinpao-an, are captured, you will have the initiative on the whole chessboard." [11] The Chinese idiom used by Mao at the end of this sentence is *"ch'üan-chü chieh huo-le,"* in literal translation, "the whole situation will be living," an expression which sounds bizarre to the Western reader but which corresponds to a common wei-ch'i idiom.[12]

These references to wei-ch'i in the writings of Mao Tse-tung serve to increase the validity of the hypothesis that wei-ch'i is an important, if little recognized, model of the Maoist system of strategy. Genuine confirmation of this thesis must, however, rest not on a few passages of Mao Tse-tung but on more detailed historical verification. Use of wei-ch'i as analogue and key to Chinese Communist insurgent strategy must, therefore, begin with analytic consideration of its historical archetype: the Communist insurgency in China from 1927 to 1949. Without such analysis, many valuable parallels to more recent applications of the Maoist strategy will be lost; and important "suppressed premises" of currently applied Communist strategy in the Chinese mold will remain undiscovered.

7

With these observations in mind, the first step of wei-ch'i analysis should consist of mapping the developing strategic situation in China during the Communist insurgency upon an imaginary wei-ch'i board: as a wei-ch'i game lasting twenty-two years and extending throughout China. In view of the extensive co-ordination by the Chinese Communists of political and military operations, such a mapping should be political as well as military. Second, the strategy of the Chinese Communists—at least as practiced by Mao Tse-tung and his associates—must be compared with the general principles of wei-ch'i strategy. Finally, upon the basis of congruences so obtained, the reasons for Chinese Communist insurgent success must be compared with the reasons for victory in a wei-ch'i game.

The revelations of the Cultural Revolution of the late 1960's—in particular, Maoist attacks upon Liu Shao-ch'i and others—have retroactively projected a considerably less unified picture of the Chinese Communist movement in its insurgent era than had previously been inferred by Western scholars. Despite the likelihood that these revelations have been exaggerated for tactical ends, this modified image cannot be entirely disregarded, and for this reason caution must be exercised in writing the strategic history of the Chinese Communist movement. As long as we keep in mind that the wei-ch'i analogy is a model of reality and not the reality itself, however, we need not pay undue attention to the existence of factionalism.

Application of wei-ch'i as an analogic model need not, moreover, be limited to China and to the pre-1949 Chinese Communist insurgency. It is also fruitful to apply the wei-ch'i analogue to post-1950 insurgent actions in Southeast Asia. While, even as in the case of the Chinese Communist insurgency, such application is more valuable for comprehending important patterns and for determining Communist objectives than for predicting the tactical implementation of those objectives, nevertheless use of wei-ch'i as an analytic approach does have heuristic value. Attempts on the part of the People's Republic of China to influence Indonesia might have been predicted as early as 1961 by use of wei-ch'i analysis and in the light of the development of events in Vietnam, as might have been the policy of the Chinese Communists toward the Indian subcontinent. On a smaller strategic scale, Maoist motifs influenced Communist strategy in South Vietnam in the 1960's, and thus that strategy is susceptible of the type of wei-ch'i analysis proposed above for the Chinese revolution.

Application of a wei-ch'i point of view to Maoist strategy past and present must and should be partial: both in structure and in strategy, every game has fewer variables than has war. Nor would a "game" as complex as war be of use in understanding war; its complexity would eliminate its function as guide and key to the social phenomenon of violent conflict. However, despite limitations of the wei-ch'i approach, application of the insights provided by the strategy of the game to the theory and practice of Maoist revolution does provide a methodology, even if only a preliminary one, by which to view in retrospect and to predict in advance the dynamics of Chinese Communist strategy.

The story has been told of four mice who lived in a barn.[13] Each was accustomed to view through a different knothole the farm animals housed in the barn. As a result, one mouse saw only the side of a cow; one, its front; the third, its rear; and the fourth, its back. These different perspectives gave rise to endless arguments among the four mice, each claiming that its own point of view provided the only correct description of what a cow looked like.

The function of the wei-ch'i analogy is to provide one knothole through which to view the Maoist cow.

●

ONE

THE GAME OF WEI-CH'I

A brief description for the purpose of politico-military analysis of an ancient highly abstract Asian game creates problems of presentation and organization comparable to those encountered by the first mathematical political scientists. On the one hand, a description of the structure and strategy of wei-ch'i adequate to satisfy a competent player of the game would be book-length and boring to the general reader; conversely, a brief description of wei-ch'i suitable for the non-initiate would, in all probability, distort the principles of the game and prove of little help in subsequent military/wei-ch'i analysis.

For these reasons, this chapter is a compromise combining a fairly full description of some salient aspects of wei-ch'i theory with as few detailed examples as possible. The aim is to stress the spirit of wei-ch'i rather than its technology.

THE STRUCTURE OF WEI-CH'I

Wei-ch'i is a two-person game, a board game, and a game of strategy; that is to say, it is, like chess, a purely intellectual game in which chance and physical dexterity play no part.

The board takes the form of a simple, square grid, usually formed from nineteen horizontal and nineteen vertical lines equidistantly spaced. A board of customary size, therefore, contains 361 intersections. Nine of the intersections are conventionally indicated as shown in Diagram 1 to serve as reference points. Other grid sizes are also used, the most common being 8 × 8, 13 × 13, and 17 × 17. It has been claimed that the strategic combinations posible on a 23 × 23 or larger board would be beyond the range of the human mind.[1]

Wei-ch'i is played with black and white pieces variously called "stones" or "men." At the start of the game, the board is empty, unless a handicap has been given. Turns alternate between Black and White, with Black playing first. On each turn one stone is placed upon any vacant intersection. The number of stones allotted to each player (181 to Black, 180 to White) for a 19 × 19 size of board is such that—for practical purposes—neither side will ever be lacking men.[2] Once played, a stone is never moved (unless *re*moved when captured).

Often, however, when there is marked difference in the skill of the players, the weaker player may have a handicap. Contrary to accepted general usage of the term, "handicap" here indicates an artificial *advantage* given to the inferior player. Taking the Black stones, he places several in a predetermined pattern on the board before the game begins,

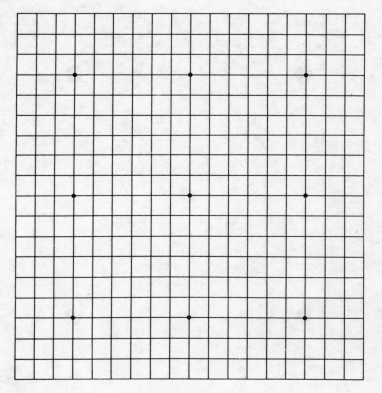

DIAGRAM 1

the number of those so placed being proportional to the estimated skill differential of the opponents. The stronger player then takes the White stones and plays first. In practice, the size of the handicap ranges from a minimum of two stones to a customary maximum of nine. A five-stone handicap is illustrated in Diagram 2.[3]

When two or more stones of one color are placed in position to form a connected chain, they are considered a single unit and are called a "group." (Stones are considered con-

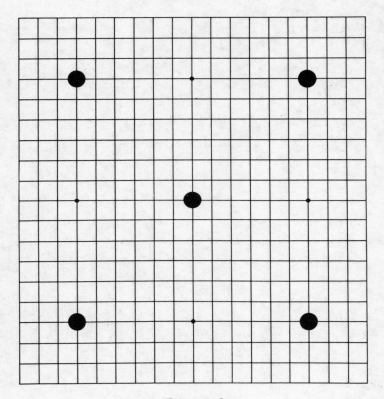

DIAGRAM 2

nected when they adjoin one another on a line, but not if they adjoin one another diagonally.) Stones of one color which are not connected but which can be connected at the will of the corresponding player may be called a "collection." [4] In Diagram 3, A and B are groups, since they form connected units. C is a collection: if Black plays at p, White can connect at q, and vice versa.

There are two objectives in wei-ch'i: control of territory and capture of hostile stones. In practice, as will become

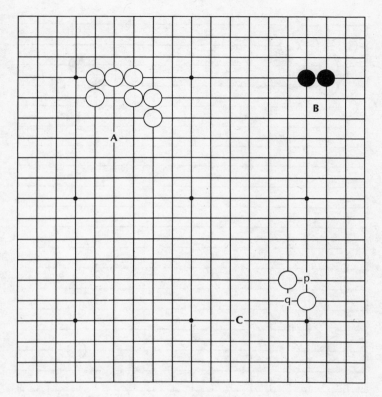

DIAGRAM 3

clear in later discussion, these two objectives are highly connected in the strategy of the game, capture of enemy pieces normally leading to acquisition of new territory, and construction of territorial bases often—but not invariably—contributing to future captures.

"Territory" may be defined as intersections impregnably surrounded by the stones of one or the other side. More formally, a territory is a connected set of empty intersections surrounded so tightly by the stones of one side

15

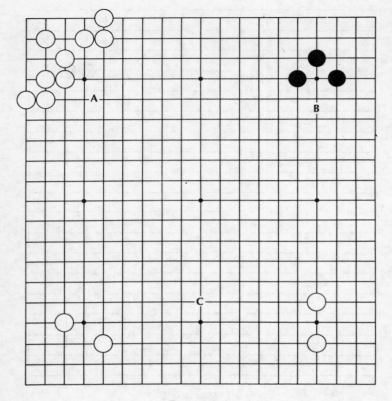

DIAGRAM 4

that attack from without by the stones of the other side
would not reduce the size of the territory; attack from
within would result in the capture of the attacking stones;
and a combined attack from within and from without would
also fail. During the process of forming territory, one side
may encircle vacant intersections in such a way that their
ultimate transformation into territory for that side is probable but not certain. Such intersections may be designated

16

"potential territory." Another wei-ch'i concept related to territory is that of "sphere of influence." This wei-ch'i term is not radically different from the same term used in politics and indicates a set of intersections under the definite hegemony of one side or the other, though not sufficiently so as to be labeled its potential territory. In Diagram 4, collection A encircles a territory in conjunction with the edges of the board; B, a potential territory; while the separated stones at C create a sphere of influence (for White) along the lower side of the board.

In general, one side captures a hostile stone or group by playing his stones on all directly adjacent intersections. Single stones in a group may be taken only by the capture, that is, the encirclement, of the entire group. If a stone or group is tangent on one or more sides to the edge of the board, encirclement on the board side only is necessary for capture. In the upper left corner of Diagram 5, for example, Black can capture the White group if he plays at p. Captured stones are removed from the board.

If a group under attack encircles one or more intersections, then its capture by the opponent necessitates encirclement both from within and from without. In Diagram 5 B, therefore, Black must play at q before he can capture the White group. In some situations, however, attempts to encircle a group from within may result only in the capture of the attacking stones. In Diagram 5 C, if White plays at r, his stone will not complete the encirclement of the Black group but will be itself surrounded and simultaneously captured. A similar result would ensue if White were to play at s. In such cases, therefore, the structure of the attacked group makes capture impossible, and equilibrium between encircler and encircled is necessarily attained. Even masters occasionally make mistakes in deciding whether or not a group is uncapturable: to acquire a moderate degree of

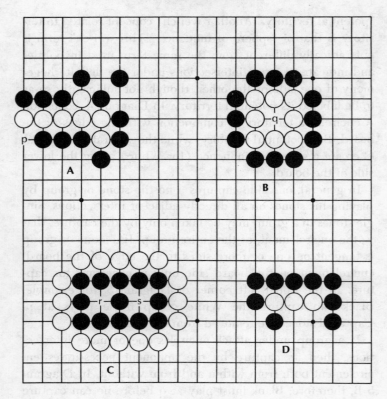

DIAGRAM 5

skill in this facet of the game demands great positional intuition and long practice. Further complex ramifications of the principles of capture are irrelevant to subsequent comparative analysis and may be found in any competent wei-ch'i text.[5]

Often stones or groups which the defender knows to be hopelessly encircled are abandoned not only by the defender but also by the attacker. The advantage for the former is that he does not add to his losses by continuing to prosecute an already hopeless defense; for the latter, that

18

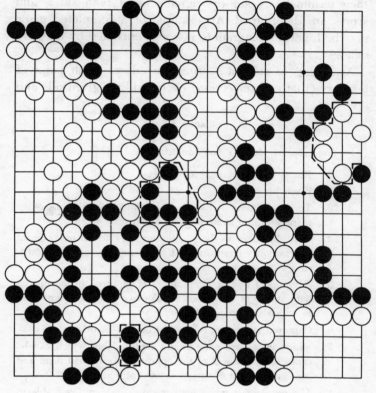

DIAGRAM 6

Source: Adapted from *The Game of Go* by Lester and Elizabeth Morris (n.p.:
The American Go Association).

he does not fill up a potential territory and lose the initiative
in other parts of the board. Such stones or groups are called
"dead." In Diagram 5 D, for instance, White's group cannot
escape from Black's encirclement and is consequently regarded as dead.[6]

Eventually in the course of a wei-ch'i game all possible
territory is encircled by one side or the other, and both sides
have captured and killed as many stones as possible. Play is

19

then terminated upon the agreement of both sides, and scores are determined. An example of a completed game may be found in Diagram 6. (Groups encircled by lines are dead.) [7]

According to current scoring procedures, each point of territory (that is, intersection) encircled by a given side and

TABLE I

(1) *The rules of wei-ch'i (no-handicap)*

1. Empty board at start of game.
2. Black plays first.
3. Turns alternate between Black and White and consist of play of one stone only on any vacant intersection.
4. The objectives of both sides are (a) to encircle vacant intersections (territory); (b) to capture or kill hostile stones.
5. A group of one or more stones is captured by occupying with stones of the opposite color every board intersection to which the group adjoins.
6. Captured stones are removed from the board.
7. Stones which are not actually captured but which can be captured at the will of the opponent are termed dead and count at the end of the game as captured.
8. The game ends when neither side considers itself able to gain further territory or to kill or capture additional enemy stones.
9. The score of a side is the sum of the number of intersections of territory which it has encircled and the number of stones captured or killed by the end of the game.
10. The side with the higher score wins.

(2) *Handicap modifications of the rules*

1'. The weaker player takes the Black stones and places several in a pre-determined pattern on the board before the game begins.
2'. White plays first.

20

each hostile stone captured or killed by that side counts one point in its total score. The side with the greater number of points wins.[8]

A summary of wei-ch'i rules may be found in Table I. A glossary of the few technical wei-ch'i terms used in this work is provided at the end of this volume.

THE STRATEGY OF WEI-CH'I

In part because of the large size of the conventional board and the large number of moves in the average game, wei-ch'i strategy is extraordinarily complex and subtle. The complexity and subtlety are further compounded by the highly abstract nature of the game. The pieces are not representational; nor is the board. As a result, the strategic patterns and potentialities of a specific wei-ch'i position are seldom apparent to the beginner. An early Western commentator on the game has summarized the novice's dilemma:

> . . . the beginning of the game [is] almost incomprehensible to one who has not studied it thoroughly. The two players seem to place their men at haphazard, now in one corner of the board and now in another; it looks rather as if they were trying to form pretty figures than trying to circumvent each other. It is only after a good many men have been placed that the object of the game begins to show itself in the play, and then gradually one perceives that those men which seemed played without any offensive or defensive purpose are all useful, and that they were placed originally to act as outposts for the territories which it was foreseen would be formed around them, or as posts of observation to annoy the enemy.[9]

In particular, the beginner frequently does not know which of his groups are dead, which living—a question basic to competent play.

The difficulty of wei-ch'i strategy has led, as in the case of chess, to vigorous development of wei-ch'i theory. The study of wei-ch'i in East Asia—in China, Japan, and, to a lesser extent, Korea—has a history of at least two thousand years; writings on wei-ch'i can be traced back for over a millennium. Because of this long history of wei-ch'i scholarship, it is only natural that many detailed treatises on the game have been compiled, some even more exhaustive than Western chess analyses. Following the example of their Asian counterparts, Western-language works on wei-ch'i have also tended toward complexity, plunging the beginning student immediately into the intricacies of board and corner openings, of extensions and connections. In this orientation toward detail, however, to which almost all Western-language works on wei-ch'i beyond the level of primers have been subject, many of the general patterns and principles of the game have remained suppressed premises, tacitly adhered to but not explicitly mentioned. In particular, among these premises are three structural characteristics basic to the motifs of the game's higher strategy: wei-ch'i is a protracted game; it is a "war of jigsaw pattern"; and it is a game in which victory and defeat are relative phenomena. Briefly, these three aspects may be called the time, space, and conflict dimensions of wei-ch'i.

The long duration of the average wei-ch'i game—between 200 and 300 moves—derives from the combined effects of two factors: a large board and a relatively slow rate of play. As previously mentioned, the standard wei-ch'i board has a total of 361 intersections, nearly six times as many as the squares on a chess board. And, whereas in some board games all pieces on the board may be moved on a given turn, in wei-ch'i only one stone may be played.[10] The strategic implications of the slow tempo resulting from these two factors are dual. Although one player may be defeated tactically in one part of the board, he may recover his position by strategic out-maneuvering of his opponent. In the best-known Western board games of strategy, chess and checkers, on the other hand, a single mistake in tactics is—given optimal play on the part of the opponent—fatal to the blunderer. Conversely, only a wei-ch'i strategy which takes into consideration the long-term outcomes of all the tactical combats on the board can ensure wei-ch'i victory, since a policy oriented toward local success often leads to a strategic debacle. By contrast to the orientation of Western strategy to realization of a single decisive tactical engagement, the concept of tactical success leading to strategic victory is alien to the spirit of wei-ch'i. In language familiar to the student of Maoist military dialectics, although the game may have its battles of quick decision, wei-ch'i is essentially a protracted war; and the deviationist theory which rejects this truth places in jeopardy not only the outcome of tactical engagements but also the total conflict.

The second characteristic of wei-ch'i structure with strategic implications is, as Mao Tse-tung has observed, the resemblance of a game in progress to a half-completed jigsaw puzzle or to a half-effaced mosaic, at once complicated and indefinite.[11] Although such comparison may be exaggerated, wei-ch'i formations tend, in fact, to be structurally nonlinear or, more precisely, discontinuous: the Black and White pieces are not grouped into two relatively continuous lines, each seeking to push the other back or to outflank the opponent. This structural component of discontinuity derives from at least two of the rule-components of wei-ch'i. First, the board is blank, or nearly so, at the beginning of the game, and stones may thereafter be placed on any vacant board intersection. Consequently, there is no restriction on the ability of either player to conduct warfare in the enemy's rear, to play his stones deep in hostile spheres of influence or behind any emerging "front line." Second, the encircling mode of capture creates complex patterns of encirclement and counterencirclement and induces the development of mutually discontinuous groups: wei-ch'i encirclement can seldom be realized by eccentric maneuver from a single group, after the fashion of a military envelopment, but rather must result from co-ordinated use of many different stones and groups often in widely separated areas of the board. As a result of these two factors—the rule of play and the rule of capture—a wei-ch'i player cannot assume the existence of a secure front line or a safe rear area. Any conscious or unconscious assumption of zones of safety will result in severe disorientation when the opponent fails to respect the inviolacy of the presumed "rear."

As significant as, and probably related to, the temporal and spatial dimensions of wei-ch'i is what may be called the conflict dimension of the game. Because of the ease with which both players can form safe groups and hence gain territory, victory in wei-ch'i is incomplete. This conflict dimension of wei-ch'i provides an additional criterion for differentiating it from many other strategic board games, among them, chess, in which victory is obtained when the opponent is forced to concede a certain vital point, set of points, or piece, or when one side loses all its pieces. One side is then totally defeated, and the other has achieved complete victory.[12] In wei-ch'i, however, victory is relative, a matter of having a greater score—basically, more territory —than one's opponent. It is only by convention—and courtesy—that the side with the higher terminal score is labeled "victor." Conversely, defeat is also relative, and the "losing" side frequently has a significant amount of secure territory to its credit.

This added relativity is due largely to the encircling mode of capture, which means that two continuous lines of stones

facing each other form a stable pattern productive of peaceful coexistence. In wei-ch'i, therefore, success is a continuum
of degrees whose measure is the score in terms of territory
and captives which a given side has realized at a given time
in the course of play. The logic, so to speak, is not Aristote-
lian but multi-valued. The would-be wei-ch'i player must
fully comprehend this fact. Throughout the course of play,
his aim should not be—to paraphrase Stonewall Jackson—to
thrash his opponent but rather to maximize his own advantage or utility, two goals which, because of the factor of
territory, are not synonymous. In its conflict dimension,
wei-ch'i is not so much like a duel as like an economic
competition for a scarce commodity.[13]

The various dimensions of wei-ch'i discussed above constitute, in a sense, the conceptual basis of the game's strategy. Actual implementation of that strategy depends, however, upon three fundamental strategic operations: gaining
territory; attack of hostile groups; and defense of one's own
groups. By the definition of territory given earlier, the first
type of operation consists of encirclement of empty intersections. According to the rules of capture, the two other processes center, respectively, around encirclement and prevention of encirclement of stones, collections, and groups.
Because of the dynamic structure of wei-ch'i as shown by
these operations, the strategy of the game revolves about
techniques of encirclement and counterencirclement.

Inasmuch as control of territory is the primary objective
of wei-ch'i, the most important principles of wei-ch'i strategy are those regulating encirclement as it relates to the surrounding of territory. In general, encirclement of desired
territory should begin by formation of a rough circle or
semicircle, consisting of a few dispersed stones, around a set
of vacant intersections (as White in Diagram 7). A frequent
error of beginners is to attempt, in the early stages of the

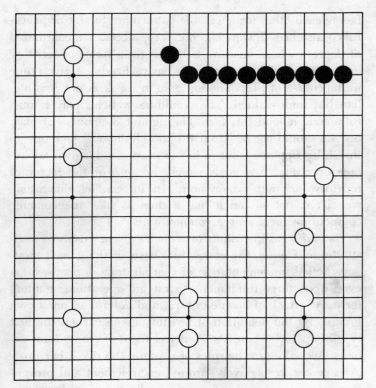

DIAGRAM 7

Source: Adapted from *How To Play Go* by Kaku Takagawa (Tokyo: Japanese Go Association). Reprinted by permission.

game, to encircle territory with a chain of tightly connected stones. The result of such a policy is certain defeat. While the beginner is concentrating on a few intersections, a competent opponent will heavily influence a large portion of the board with his stones. Although only tightly encircled intersections are the certain territory of the encircler, it is a mistake to underestimate the connective power of dispersed stones and hence the amount of potential territory which

26

they loosely encircle. In Diagram 7, White, having dispersed his first-played stones in an effective manner, dominates much of the board; whereas Black, although having a secure hold on one territory, will be able to gain little more and is in a losing position.[14]

At the same time, however, it is a fact that zones of influence as well as potential territories are vulnerable to enemy attack until such time as they are transformed into actual territory. As a result, when such regions are threatened by enemy attack, the encirclement should be tightened to meet the threat. This tightening of encirclement, however, should not be guided by the doctrine of massive retaliation but by the theory of graduated deterrence: one of the principal differences between a beginner and a master is that the master knows exactly how much to tighten the encirclement of a threatened zone of influence, whereas the beginner frequently wastes plays strengthening his defense out of proportion to the magnitude of the threat.

In view of the jigsaw patterns of wei-ch'i stressed above, it would, of course, be an error to assume that encirclement of territory proceeds in a formal, explicit, and symmetric way: that a player must first map out a complete perimeter around empty intersections and then subsequently place more stones at smaller intervals until a continuous chain is formed. On the contrary, a skillful wei-ch'i player utilizes every one of his groups, wherever they may be on the board, as a segment of a wall enclosing a possible territory; and often plans offensive and defensive operations not so much with the aim of capture or prevention of capture but with the objective of completing encirclement of a potential territory. Moreover, a competent wei-ch'i player knows how to utilize the edges of the board as an aid in encircling the maximum amount of territory. These edges form natural walls, from beyond which no hostile group can penetrate into the border area base. An efficient player, therefore, plays first near the corners, where two edges of the board do half his work for him; next, along the sides (as White in Diagram 7), where one side of the potential territory is protected by the edge of the board; and, last of all, in center regions where encirclement of territory is most difficult.[15]

Encirclement of hostile stones, though a secondary objective in wei-ch'i because of the relative difficulty of its implementation compared to acquisition of territory, is nevertheless vital to the interests of a player who wishes to capitalize on his opponent's weaknesses and mistakes. A good player will frequently make every move bear an aggressive intent, even if it is primarily territory-making, or defensive. In general, the procedure for encircling hostile stones is approximately the same as for encircling territory, though, as pointed out, its realization is more complicated owing to the virtual certainty of vigorous enemy opposition. First, encirclement should be roughly outlined in such a manner that the enemy group cannot conduct an effective breakout to safety. Next, the encirclement should be tightened, and attempts made to prevent creation by the opponent of an invincible position.

It cannot be emphasized too strongly, however, that an attempted encirclement of a strong group may be detrimental, even disastrous, to the interests of the encircler. If the bases for encirclement are unconsolidated, then a counterattack will often disconnect the encircling forces and may cause their capture. Moreover, eagerness to kill and capture has often led a novice to play his attacking stones on exterior lines right up against the stones he is trying to encircle, thus inducing a disintegrating counterattack before the offensive forces have achieved a decisive blockade.

On the whole, methods of defense in wei-ch'i are the logical converse of principles of attack. The aim of the defending player is to form a continuum of stones beyond which the opponent cannot pass; then (optimistically) to make a successful counterencirclement. In the attainment of these objectives, two techniques may be used. If the defender's position is relatively strong—that is, connected, flexible, and with a good chance of becoming ultimately invincible—he should attempt to stop the attack on the perimeter of his zone of influence by directly blocking enemy advances. (Refer to Black defense in Diagram 8 A.) [16]

If the defender's position is less consolidated, however, as is characteristic during the decisive opening and early middle game, a good player, at least temporarily, cedes a portion of his stones and influence and directs his play several intersections distant from the center of gravity of the attacking forces, thus gaining valuable time to consolidate his position before final confrontation. In Diagram 8 B-C, a simple (tactical) example of this motif is provided. (Note that the basic positions are mirror images of one another.) If Black plays 1 as shown, White should on no account directly confront this aggression by playing 2 as in 8 B: the whole flank of his position would crumble instantly, as depicted in the 8 B sequence (the block of five White stones is dead). If, however, White "withdraws" by playing 2 as shown in 8 C, then—even if Black continues his invasion as shown—Black cannot make an effective penetration into the heart of White territory. In other words, an indirect White 2 is critical in maintaining a structurally sound force deployment.[17]

Related to the attack and defense of stones and groups, and often preliminary to them, are the strategic principles surrounding connection and disconnection. In view of the jigsaw pattern of wei-ch'i, a good player, at least in the early and middle games, will refrain from tight, uneconomical connections between two separated groups. On the other

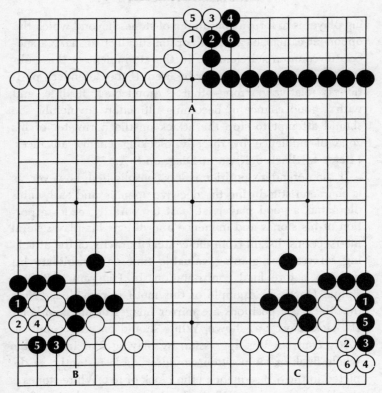

DIAGRAM 8

Source: A. Adapted from *The American Go Journal: An Anthology* (n.p.: The American Go Association). B. Developed by the author. C. *The American Go Journal: An Anthology.*

hand, he must know the art of maintaining communications in such a manner that he will be able to tighten connections if the occasion arises. In practice, the methods of developing and maintaining collections are manifold, and their mastery is an intricate study. In theory, however, the principle is simple to grasp. The defensive advantage of collections is that, if one element is attacked, other elements can come to its aid by tightening latent avenues of communication; if, however, there is some strategic reason for abandoning one element of the collection, the safety of the others need not be jeopardized. Conversely, in offensive operations, the first operational goal of the attacker should be to isolate the attacked group from possible outside support, because an otherwise successful attack on one group can often be nullified by the collective defense of several groups.

The offensive, the defensive, and—in wei-ch'i—the territory-making techniques employed in a strategic conflict form the basis of that conflict's resolution. Underlying these operational methods, however, another equally important set of principles may be delineated: briefly described, this latter set controls and regulates methods of command decision. Collectively, these principles may be termed control processes. In wei-ch'i, at least three are essential: initiative, co-ordination, and economy. Despite the seeming universality of these concepts—slightly paraphrased they may be found, for instance, in any military *Field Service Manual*— many of the characteristics of their wei-ch'i interpretations are relatively unique. It is to the control processes of wei-ch'i that we must turn, therefore, in order to complete a survey of the theoretical strategy of the game.

Perhaps the most important of the three control processes just mentioned is the wei-ch'i concept of initiative, *hsien-shou* in Chinese wei-ch'i jargon. Literally, the expression *hsien-shou* means "first hand," and it is roughly similar in connotation to the English word "initiative." One fundamental difference must, however, be grasped. In English-language military/strategic usage, the term "initiative" refers, in general, to some type of overt offensive action; and "strategic initiative" is, therefore, closely connected with the idea of strategic offensive. This intimate relation between initiative and offensive is lacking in the Chinese phrase.

31

Broadly defined, *hsien-shou* is "the situation in which a player is taking the lead in a certain part of the board, compelling his adversary to answer his moves or else sustain greater damage." [18] In other words, a *hsien-shou* move is any move which makes the succeeding move on the part of the opponent a dependent event contingent on the *hsien-shou* move and a direct reply to it.

The method of taking the lead implicit in the above definition would, therefore, include such occurrences as the threatened escape of a dead group; the possibility of a large new territory (for example, as a result of successful containment); and, as in the illustration given below, the consolidation of a base for future aggression.[19] If the concept of *hsien-shou* is at all to be coupled with that of the offensive, it must be seen as embracing a spectrum of often very subtle offensive activities extending far beyond mere threats to kill and capture enemy groups. At the same time, *hsien-shou* is not the monopoly of a player on the strategic offensive: it may be possessed by a player on the strategic defensive and even maintained by what is essentially non-offensive action.

A concrete example of the nature and value of *hsien-shou* may be found in Diagram 9 A. In the position illustrated, if it is White's move, he should play at a, capturing the Black stone, outflanking his adversary's position, and reducing his influence.[20] Suppose, however, that it is Black's turn. Then Black's play at intersection a might well force White to connect at b (otherwise, Black would play at b or c and cut White's forces in two). Hence, Black 1 at a, although defensive in form, retains *hsien-shou* because (at least within the context of the local position) White must respond or take a greater loss. Following White 2 at b, Black may play at d, thus striking at another weak point of White's position. The precise outcome of the conflict from this point cannot be as-

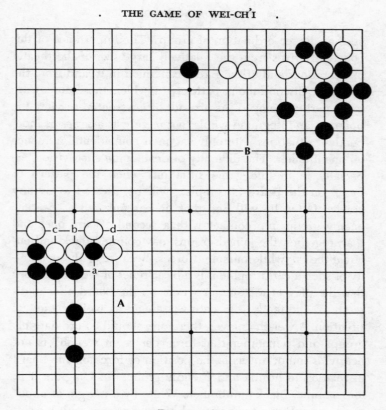

DIAGRAM 9

Source: A. Adapted from *Go Proverbs Illustrated* by Kensaku Segoe (Tokyo: Japanese Go Association). Reprinted by permission. B. Adapted from *The Game of Go* by Arthur Smith (Rutland, Vermont: Charles E. Tuttle Co., Inc.). Reprinted by permission.

certained without knowing the position of other forces on the board. In general, however, it is safe to assert that Black's maintenance of *hsien-shou* with move 1 at a, even in what might be considered a defensive situation, has laid the foundation for a large sphere of influence in the lower-left quadrant of the board.

A second control process in wei-ch'i is co-ordination;

specifically, co-ordination of groups. The importance of this concept derives from the relatively large size of the theater of operations and of the forces contained in it; and from the complex, discontinuous patterns in which those forces are customarily deployed. As a result, it is essential to view the board as an integrated whole, not merely as a series of independent situations with only vague or coincidental influence on one another. The difficulty of developing such vision, especially in middle game situations when the pattern of forces on the board is complex, will be attested to by any novice. Often he will find that he has pursued a "beaten" enemy group into contact with a second, secure one; and that, together, the joined groups may counterattack and encircle the erstwhile pursuing forces. Because of the possibility of such a catastrophe, it is a basic tenet of wei-ch'i theory that the play of a stone anywhere on the board affects, directly or indirectly, the entire strategic as well as tactical situation. A wei-ch'i player, therefore, should co-ordinate his groups and remember that force per se in wei-ch'i is not nearly as important as is the position of force on the board in relation to hostile and friendly groups. In Diagram 9 B, for example, Black outnumbers White by a margin of about two to one. By co-ordination of his two groups with his single stone in the upper right corner, however, White can manage to capture [kill] the two-stone Black group and thus hold more than half the corner. No two of the three White units alone would be sufficient for the task.[21]

One of the best modern wei-ch'i players has observed, "[Wei-ch'i] is the art of harmony." [22] The basis of harmonious play is economy. Economy in wei-ch'i involves an efficient, almost aesthetic, balance of forces, both in their internal structure and in their interrelation. By contrast to many forms of conflict in which strategic concentration is the key to success, wei-ch'i economy is based, especially in the open-

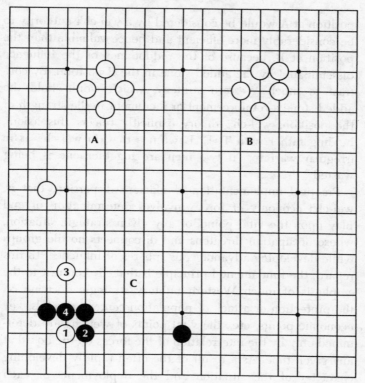

DIAGRAM 10

Source: A. Developed by the author. B. Developed by the author. C. Adapted from *The Vital Points of Go* by Kaku Takagawa (Tokyo: Japanese Go Association). Reprinted by permission.

ing, on minimization of congestion of influence produced by overconcentration of stones.[23] Both in terms of intersections influenced and of hostile stones threatened, the most economical, therefore the most efficient, patterns are those which make use of calculated dispersion of forces to maximize influence dissemination. As concrete examples, consider the two formations at the top of the board in Diagram 10. They appear to be almost identical. In fact, however, the position at A would be considered by a wei-ch'i authority to be considerably more efficient and hence valuable than the position at B, because of the redundancy of the influence disseminated by the added stone in the B position. By contrast to much Western strategy, which would hold the added stone a reinforcement or increment in the strength of the position, wei-ch'i theory explicitly rejects this axiom, holding rather with T. E. Lawrence that, in wei-ch'i as in irregular warfare, "if two men are together one is being wasted." [24]

Practical implementation of efficient dispersion, that is, wei-ch'i economy of force, involves determination of and play upon the vital points of any given strategic situation, whose occupation threatens and disconnects hostile groups while developing advantageous spheres of influence. In this regard, the fundamental principle is that, by contrast to the emphasis of much Western military/strategic doctrine on the protection or attack of population centers, capitals, key economic points, etc., the vital points of wei-ch'i are determined only by the interrelation of the forces on the board at any given time. As a result of the often rapidly developing character of the situation and the deployments of each side, the vital points of the position change frequently, and a group of stones or sphere of influence formerly considered important may be sacrificed with impunity.[25] This flexibility of play tends to convey the impression, especially when the game is between good players, that wei-ch'i is formless, even aimless in strategy. No interpretation could be farther from the truth. Constant reevaluation of the situation and of the vital points of the position is necessary for good play, and sacrifice of stones or of influence in one region in expectation of more advantageous operations elsewhere is a common motif of higher wei-ch'i strategy. In Diagram 10 C, for instance, White 1 is what may be called a "reconnaissance" play. If we then have the indicated sequence 2-4, White's corner stone will be dead, but the gambit is excellent higher strategy because, with 3, White has succeeded in reducing the shoulder of the Black sphere of influence while retaining *hsien-shou*.[26] This example is typical of a sophisticated wei-ch'i maneuver.

It may be desirable to conclude with a word of caution. To introduce a term recently fashionable in some circles of strategic analysis, wei-ch'i strategy is a branch of the art of the dialectic: the dialectic of discontinuous connections, concentrated dispersion, encircled counterencirclement, flexible inflexibility. The paradoxes of the wei-ch'i dialectic are possibly not as insoluble as those of its Hegelian counterpart. It is, however, impossible to lay down absolute canons for wei-ch'i command decisions. Human perception of optimal or—to use a term from the mathematical theory of games—minimax wei-ch'i strategy is continually changing and evolving: an example is afforded by the emergence in the 1920's of a new school of play, originated by Wu Ch'ing-yuan, which broke away from the traditional opening patterns and stressed relatively more influence toward the center of the board.[27] No summary of the principles of wei-ch'i can be exhaustive.

TWO

WEI-CH'I AND INSURGENCY:
A FORMAL ANALOGY

Detailed analogic comparison of Chinese Communist strategy with the strategy of wei-ch'i must start, as indicated in the Introduction, by explicitly setting in correspondence the basic structural elements of the two forms of conflict.[1] Such a system of correspondences cannot be proved correct. It is only intuitively justifiable, and its validity depends upon the reasonableness of the ensuing deductions. For the most part, therefore, the present treatment will develop only simple and obvious analogies. The conceptual apparatus which this chapter creates is applicable to any insurgency in a developing nation which follows the Maoist model (and, by extension, to broader spheres such as foreign policy and world revolution). However, concrete reference in the ensuing discussion will be largely limited to analysis of the 1927–1949 Chinese case.

From the point of view of relative complexity, wei-ch'i and the Chinese Communist style of revolution are widely disparate conflict systems. A total system of correspondences between each component or process of wei-ch'i and each element of insurgency is impossible. Taking advantage of the structural simplicity and flexibility of the game, however, we may to a certain extent generalize the structure of wei-ch'i. For instance, wei-ch'i in its pure form is a two-person game. However, many sides (in the sense of independent, interested actors) participated in politico-military operations in China during the 1927–49 Communist insurgency: the Communists, the Nationalists (by no means unified), the Japanese, and sundry warlords.[2] No integral or distinct element of *elementary* wei-ch'i strategy is based upon wei-ch'i's being a two-person game.[3] Therefore, in order to facilitate comparative analysis, we can conceive of extending the rules of the game to those of multi-person conflict. Such a form of generalized wei-ch'i may be termed "analogic wei-ch'i." [4]

THE CONFLICT SYSTEMS

The basic correspondence between wei-ch'i and insurgency is, of course, between their totalities as conflict systems, that is, between the course of a wei-ch'i game and the history of a politico-military insurgency. In the case of insurgencies after the Chinese Communist pattern to which our attention is specifically directed, revolution is the logical union of two interrelated but nevertheless structurally distinct levels of conflict activity: the geographic level—the level of military operations; and the human level—the level of the socio-political warfare so closely co-ordinated by the Chinese

Communists with military campaigns. For analytic purposes, therefore, the general correspondence between wei-ch'i and Chinese Communist insurgency should be divided into that between wei-ch'i and military operations and that between wei-ch'i and political, economic, and psychological conflict techniques.[5]

These correspondences between wei-ch'i and the military and political aspects of nationwide insurgency do not, however, preclude similar correspondences between a wei-ch'i game and sub-conflicts properly contained within the totality of the revolution. For example, it is relevant to consider Chinese Communist operations against the Nationalist armies in Manchuria between 1946 and 1948 as an independent sub-game of the over-all Chinese Communist insurgency. In general, a certain military and/or political campaign or operation may be considered an independent game insofar—and only insofar—as it is both strategically independent from operations simultaneously taking place in adjoining theaters *and* strategically important to the national situation. The key is strategy: many congruences analyzed below tend to lose their validity when applied in the sphere of tactics (where, for example, the contrast between the mobility of military units and the immobility of wei-ch'i stones stands out most clearly).

THE SIDES

All games and sub-games of a given insurgency are generated and conducted by a number of frequently competing, sometimes co-operating, political interests. In general, any strategically significant group of individuals bound together by common political and personal goals and organizational affiliations may be placed in correspondence with a wei-ch'i side and treated as such in the development of strategic analogies. In contrast to the monadic character of the wei-ch'i side, however, the military and political sides involved in the 1927–49 Chinese insurgency in particular and in many other revolutions have often lacked internal cohesion.[6] In the Chinese case, this observation applies especially to the warlords and their subordinates, whose disunity and opportunism have attracted the attention of even Western military historians.[7] Identification of a given socially, politically, or organizationally connected group of individuals with a side in the wei-ch'i sense can, therefore, be only approximate and must be based on a posteriori political evaluation. The entire history of the 1946–49 Chinese civil war, for example, is colored by the constant non-co-operation of Nationalist commanders nominally acting in a common cause. Allowances for this type of situation must therefore be made in subsequent military/wei-ch'i comparative analysis.

THE THEATER OF OPERATIONS

To each game and sub-game of insurgent action, whether military or political in character, there corresponds a unique board which determines the extent of the operations of the game. The theater of operations, or board, of a military game may be considered to be a physical area: province, river valley, nation-state, and so on; that of a political game, a definite human population.

On the largest scale in the 1927–49 Chinese revolution, the military board of the Communists was the geographic extent of China, especially the traditional eighteen provinces; the human board was the population of the country. All boards of military and political sub-games were contained within these maximal boards. Such a complex system of interrelated boards and sub-boards might be projected in

41

analogic wei-ch'i by placing in conjunction a group of wei-ch'i boards with special rules for play and interboard capture.

The boundaries of sub-boards of insurgency can be determined by two types of criteria, or a combination of them: natural criteria, that is, natural obstacles, ethno-linguistic differences (for population boards), etc., all of which serve objectively to differentiate one board from another; and artificial criteria, such as military zones or administrative boundaries, which may or may not correspond to objective realities.[8] Thus, for example, China as a whole forms a natural board, both political and military, bounded as it is on the east by the Pacific; on the west and south by the Himalayan mountains and their offshoots; and to the north by deserts and other natural barriers.[9] Historical tradition and the written language have also served to define China as a natural board on the human level. In contrast, South Vietnam constitutes an artificial board. On the military level, as Communist infiltration in the 1960's from nearby Laos and Cambodia amply indicated, its edges are open and fluid; while its population—Vietnamese and Montagnard, Buddhist and Catholic, Cao Dai and Hoa Hao—forms a complex of overlapping natural human sub-boards with little or no psychological or cultural integration.

On the human level, a board is composed of intersections which may without artificiality be identified with individuals or, as may occasionally be useful, with groups of individuals. In wei-ch'i strategy, however, the importance of intersections lies not in their separate nature—they are only abstract points—but in their structural interrelation as constituents of a wei-ch'i board. It would be precious to draw lengthy parallels between the way in which intersections make up the wei-ch'i board and the manner in which men form human groups. Nevertheless, it should be clear that

42

(qualitative) propositions about encirclements on the wei-ch'i board, for example, may be translated into comparable statements concerning human social interactions and communication nets.[10] One particular concept related to wei-ch'i board structure deserves closer consideration in development of our analogy: the notion of distance from the edge of the board on the part of a given intersection or set of intersections. The key is inaccessibility.

The strategic importance of this wei-ch'i concept was set forth briefly in the preceding chapter: near the edge of the board, groups can more easily form territory than in the center and, in particular, can more easily become invincible. (The complete significance of the edge, however, is more complex and will be dealt with in the following chapter.) Because of the strategically pivotal character of the edge of the wei-ch'i board, it is important to find a meaningful analogue in the theater of insurgent political action. Clearly the physical distance of a given individual from the periphery of a given natural board, as here defined, has no direct strategic significance. Even less reasonable would be a measure based upon distance from the boundary of an *artificial* board.

As a more natural alternative, we propose to identify the edge of the human board with the lower socio-economic strata of a society. The analogic measure of a given individual's (intersection's) distance from the edge is proportional to that individual's social position and economic privilege. In this way, the wei-ch'i concept can be effectively mapped onto the class structure around the analysis and exploitation of which much of Maoist theory revolves.[11] The assumption of a linear socio-economic ordering is, of course, an approximation but, statistically, a defensible one in the context of the type of societies in which leaders of Maoist-type revolution contemplate operating. Subsequently in the development of the wei-ch'i thesis we shall operationally justify this particular analogy by demonstrating that the respective roles of the edge and center intersections in wei-ch'i are comparable to those of mass and elite in the Maoist revolutionary model.[12]

On the human level, individuals constitute a natural and efficient biological analogue to intersections in wei-ch'i. However, on a level of primary importance in this analysis, the military level, no such precise image of the wei-ch'i concept is forthcoming. It might, of course, be possible to project intersections on a given map region by superimposing on it an arbitrary system of rectangular coordinates, much as is done by artillery control specialists; but the subjectivity of scale of such a projection would render its employment difficult. In this analysis, therefore, we seek to make the weight of the comparison between wei-ch'i and Maoist warfare rest upon propositions whose validity does not depend upon specification of "intersections." [13]

Absence of an objective counterpart for wei-ch'i intersections on the military level does not, however, mean that we should not define an analogic measure of distance from the edge of the board. In fact, possession of such a measure is basic to our study of the Chinese Communist territorial concept in ensuing chapters. One possibility, of course, is measurement of the distance as a simple geometric quantity. This alternative is, however, rendered artificial by the indeterminateness of the board from whose edge distance is to be measured: no geographic theater of operations, however natural, is other than a relative construct. To a battalion of mechanized infantry in trucks, a rice paddy is the edge of the board; a tank unit may be able to traverse the paddy but cannot climb the mountain which adjoins it; and foot soldiers who can climb the mountain could not necessarily cross the Himalayas in mid-winter, a feat, in turn, simple for a squadron of heavy bombers.

We solve the dilemma by presenting an index of nearness to the edge of the board which takes into account ambiguities in board determination. Although several alternatives suggest themselves, the most straightforward procedure is to base military nearness-to-the-edge upon topographic criteria: the distance-from-the-edge of a region is identified with the military mobility which the terrain of the area permits. This definition harmonizes with our characterization of the boundaries of a natural geographic-level board as geographical obstacles and provides a workable formula for measuring the analogical characteristic in question. Cities and lines of communication form the centermost region of the board; plains or fields, a region intervening between edge and center; and mountainous hinterlands, the intersections nearest the edge, since it is in these regions that military forces have minimum mobility. There is strong positive correlation between our military and political characterizations of nearness-to-edge: for, in a developing nation, the peasants, who form the bulk of the lower register of the socio-economic scale, tend to live away from heavily urbanized areas and hence, by our definition, toward the edges of the geographic natural board.

THE FORCES

On the human level, a given individual may be termed a stone of a given side at a given time if he is engaged in systematic political activity on its behalf and is working to advance its interests. On the geographical level, a stone is an individual or group of individuals operating for a side in a military or paramilitary capacity, that is, both willing and able to attempt physical coercion of stones hostile to that side. In practice, the only military stones which we will consider are organized military units. Because, as previously stressed, no objective coordinate system for a military board can be realistically constructed, stones may be military units of an arbitrary size. In concrete analysis, however, it is necessary to set a mean size for stones in such a way that the number of stones on the revolutionary board at any one time is roughly commensurate with the population of its wei-ch'i counterpart: too large a number would render wei-ch'i strategic analysis impractical, while too few would cause oversimplification.

Since there are many different degrees of quality on the part of military and political stones, we must distinguish in concrete cases among different values of stones, depending on such variables as dedication, organization, and technology. Such distinctions might be projected in an analogic form of wei-ch'i by introducing several types of pieces, with special rules which make easier the encirclement and capture of the qualitatively less valuable stones.

In insurgency, military and political stones may be played in two quite different ways. On the one hand, new stones may come into being by recruitment of new adherents to a cause, or by the assignment of elements in existing forces to form new operational amalgams ("force tailoring" in modern military jargon). This is the play of stones in its most literal sense. On the other hand, overland movement (horizontal mobility) of military or political forces can also be interpreted in many instances as a sequence of wei-ch'i plays. Advances are wei-ch'i extensions toward the enemy; retreats, extensions away from the opponent. It is frequently possible to minimize the effects of mobility because one is considering, for the most part, revolutionary situations with a gradual tempo of progressive but semi-static strategic development rather than blitzkrieg with swiftly shifting and recombining patterns of force.[14]

A complementary way of looking at the mobility which military units possess is to identify this factor with certain subtle elements of wei-ch'i's unadapted structure. In this connection, we may note the following comment from a Western textbook on the game:

> The influence or value of a stone after the first few opening moves is a function of what we might term its mobility. Near a corner a stone can usually be developed only in one or two directions, and near the side of the board in two or three directions, while near the middle of the board a stone will frequently have the choice between extending in four directions. The stone has more mobility in the centre because its freedom of extension is not yet hampered by other stones scattered in the corners and along the edges of the board.[15]

This type of strategic argument sets up a counterpoise to the dominantly edge-oriented strategy of wei-ch'i, even as Maoist theory argues for the co-ordination of mobile with guerrilla warfare.

Objectives and the Structure of Their Attainment

The objective of territory in wei-ch'i might be compared on the human level to that of influencing individuals (intersections) to support a given side and on the geographic level to the aim of controlling land (territory). It is true, of course, that no military-level territory can be as logically and absolutely irreducible as its wei-ch'i counterpart; but in practice this reservation has little significance, because in the active course of a wei-ch'i game few positions are completely secure.

47

Similarly, the negative objective of capture of stones can be projected on the human level as the influencing (by any means other than direct violence) of enemy stones so as to cause those stones to refrain from further opposing action; such means may be bribery, psychological pressure, or political propaganda. Capture on the military level may correspondingly be defined as destruction of hostile stones: physical annihilation. Using the weakened definition of military stones as organized units, however, disintegration of hostile military forces as organized units may also be termed military capture. In a similar spirit, we identify surrender (of a military force) with the removal of a dead group at the end of a wei-ch'i game. For obvious reasons, however, incautious attempts to label as "dead" encircled or otherwise incapacitated military units would be ill-advised.

This matrix of theoretical concepts, in conjunction with that developed in the preceding section, corresponds in large part to well-known distinctions in unconventional warfare terminology.[16] Thus, for example, what we have called acquiring territory (on the political level) corresponds in essence to *l'action psychologique,* defined by French theorists of *la guerre révolutionnaire* as political action directed against friendly or neutral forces; and this action must be differentiated from the (political) capture of enemy stones, which is nothing other than *la guerre psychologique,* political action directed against the supporters of the enemy. Of course, the semantics cannot be carried too far: the difference between the stones and the territory of a given side is occasionally blurred, though presumably the stones are active elements with definite organizational affiliations as, for example, with the Communist party.

Finally, it should be noted that, according to the definitions given in the first paragraph of this section, military units may also be political spheres of influence—and not necessarily of their own side alone—and hence may be attacked by political means; and, conversely, political stones and territory can be captured and encircled by military methods. Both corollaries are important in understanding the foundations of the Chinese Communist system of revolution.

STRATEGIC INFORMATION

In developing a systematic analogy between wei-ch'i and insurgency, we have so far confined discussion to the "classic" elements of strategic structure: sides, forces, objectives, and so forth. Given the sophisticating influence of game theory on social science, however, it is necessary to go beyond tradition and to raise, at least briefly, issues related to the state of information (the information set) of a given conflict actor at a given time.[17]

Wei-ch'i belongs to that class of conflicts labeled by game theorists "perfect information" games: namely, games in which, on any given turn, each player knows all moves anterior to that turn and hence comprehends fully all elements in the existing situation. In any form of military or political conflict, on the other hand, no side can have optimal information regarding the capabilities and activities of the participants, even of its own forces. The fog of battle is proverbial.

Generalizations like these cannot, however, be employed to shape our interpretations of reality. Certain features of Maoist revolutionary warfare effectively minimize the information gap between the Maoist form of conflict and wei-ch'i. In the development of the wei-ch'i hypothesis, the principal concern is with the Chinese Communist decision-maker. According to the model of revolution which Mao Tse-tung presents, a determining characteristic of the insurgent side is to be the all-embracing range of the in-

TABLE II

Generic designation	Wei-ch'i concept	Structural component of insurgency	
		Geographic level	*Human level*
Conflict system	Wei-ch'i game	Military operations	Non-violent strategic activity
Actor	Side (Black or White)	Politico-military side or interest	Population of theater
Conflict space	Board	Theater of operations	Natural or administrative division
Boundary of conflict space	Boundary (of board)		
Unit of conflict space	Intersection	Indeterminate homogeneous geographic area	Individual or (human) group
Distance from boundary of conflict space	Distance from edge of board	Degree of mobility (afforded by terrain of given unit of conflict space)	Distance from bottom of linear socio-economic scale
Unit of force	Stone	Individual soldier or military unit	Individual cadre, core political activist, or group thereof
Zone of control	Territory and influence	Geographic territorial control; base area	Non-core supporters of side
Elimination of force units	Capture (of stones)	Annihilation and/or disintegration of hostile military units; more broadly, violent elimination of hostile forces	Conversion or disaffection of hostile groups; more broadly, non-violent elimination of hostility

formation set possessed at all times by insurgent political leaders and military commanders. In more picturesque language,

> The enemy stands as on a lighted stage; from the darkness around him, thousands of unseen eyes intently study his every move, his every gesture.[18]

Granted that this model is only normative, both in China and in Vietnam, model and reality have frequently coincided. The strategic intelligence which the Chinese Communist commanders possessed, except in the early phases of the revolution, was sufficiently extensive as to exclude serious incomparabilities with wei-ch'i situations.

●

───────

THREE

THE KIANGSI PERIOD

In underlying structure, wei-ch'i is pre-eminently a contest of position. Because of this fundamental feature of the game, application of its strategic concepts to the board of revolution appropriately begins with study of a positional principle: "that there is," as it has been phrased, "a logical progression of occupation: first the corners, then the sides, and finally the center." [1] Analysis of this wei-ch'i axiom—it might be more tersely labeled the "principle of the-edge-of-the-board"—in its applications both to Communist and to anti-Communist strategic behavior is the central theme of the present chapter.

Our treatment starts in 1927, a date to which the Chinese Communists retrospectively ascribe the birth of the Red Army and of the "hot"—that is, the military—phase of the history of their insurgency. Prior to that year, though the Communist party of China had been in existence since 1921, the operations of the movement were relatively ineffective in realizing grass-roots organization of the masses and in developing independent bases for revolutionary struggle.[2]

The first strategic phase of the Chinese Communist revolution relevant to this study began in 1927 and lasted until 1935. Because during most of this period the capital of the central Communist revolutionary base area was located at the city of Juichin in Kiangsi province (Map 1), this strategic stage of the insurgency is conventionally labeled the Kiangsi period.

The aim of the present study being strategic analysis rather than intellectual, political, or even military history, we sketch only the general contours of this epoch of recent Chinese history. The story of the period is largely one of regionalism, factionalism, and political disaffection: superficial integration in the late Ch'ing period was followed by a period of interdynastic chaos.

The political and military situation in China in 1927, at the beginning of the period under consideration, was a patchwork of interlocking and overlapping zones of control and influence of a large number of competing parties and interests, many of which may be grouped under the term "warlord." Thus, for instance, one individual controlled Manchuria, another Shansi province in north China (refer to Map 2); and so on. The most ultimately durable of all non-Communist political factions in China during this period was, of course, that of the Nationalists under Chiang Kai-shek. In 1926–27, this side was expanding its sphere of influence northward from Canton in south China in what is known as the Northern Expedition. At first, the Nationalists numbered the Communists among their allies in this endeavor, but, in the spring of 1927, Chiang decided to break with the Communists and instituted a series of purges lasting throughout the latter half of that year.

Following the Nationalist-Communist split, the weakened Communists also divided. The Party's Central Committee remained underground in Shanghai and, on the whole, followed official Comintern directives which stressed proletarian revolution. Another group of Communists, however, led by Mao Tse-tung and Chu Teh, meanwhile created a revolutionary base in a power vacuum which existed in mountainous areas of southeast China and applied with considerable success the unorthodox formula of politico-military action later embodied in the so-called "thought of Mao Tsetung." This initial division of Communist strategic policy proved a constant source of intraparty discord throughout the remainder of the Kiangsi period, even after the Central Committee moved to Kiangsi about 1932. More detailed commentary on strategic aspects of this dissension is given below.[3]

For the eight years which followed 1927, the over-all political and military pattern in China evolved from that prevailing in 1927 but without noteworthy change. The Nationalists gradually extended their hegemony over most parts of China, here allying with one warlord, there fighting another. Eventually, by 1935, the forces of Chiang Kai-shek had gained some semblance of authority over the provinces of China proper. Meanwhile, various soviet bases like that in Kiangsi developed, often quite independently, in scattered regions of the country (see Map 3).[4] These bases underwent almost continuous attacks by both warlord and Nationalist forces, which evidently shared the feeling that their security was threatened more by social revolutionaries than by one another. By 1935, the Nationalists—in part, because of anti-wei-ch'i tendencies in Communist strategy (analyzed below)—had succeeded in "clearing and holding" the major

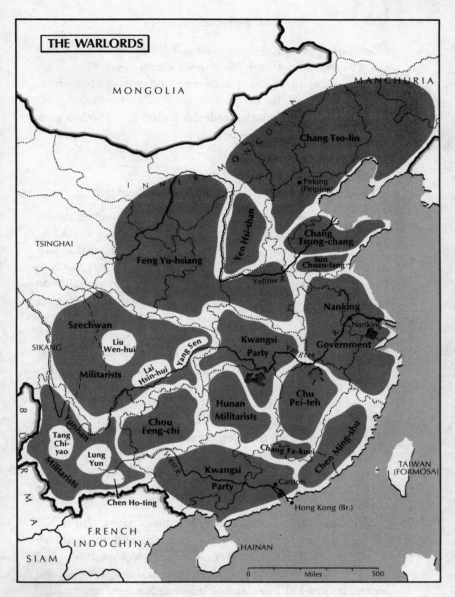

MAP 2

Source: From "The Kuomintang and National Unification, 1928–1931" by Melville T. Kennedy, Jr. (unpublished dissertation, Harvard University). The original map appeared as an enclosure to dispatch No. 1413 dated March 1, 1928, from the United States Legation, Peking, China, State Department File 893.00/9853, National Archives, Record Group No. 59.

Communist territorial stronghold in Kiangsi. With the fall of the Central Soviet and most other Communist base areas and the subsequent Long March of Communist forces from southeast China to another base in the northwest, the Kiangsi period may be considered ended and another strategic phase of insurgency begun.

CHINA, 1927: STRATEGY AND GEOPOLITICS

During the Kiangsi period of Chinese Communism, countless sides and factions throughout China—provincial, regional, and national—were the spectators and participants in a wei-ch'i game: a wei-ch'i game whose aim was the control of geographic and human territory, and the annihilation of the politico-military stones of rival players. The number of these sides was especially large in 1927, but it decreased as the Nationalists gradually allied with or eliminated their principal competitors. Although in 1927, as subsequent Nationalist victories served to indicate, no side was in firm possession of a significant portion of either the human or the geographic board of China, nevertheless many players had a considerable number of stones and widespread influence. The competitors of the Communists in 1927 might, therefore, be appropriately compared to handicap players in a handicap multi-player wei-ch'i game; and the Chinese Communists themselves, to White, that is, to the player without a handicap.

Although there were many handicap sides, from the wei-ch'i point of view both the political and the military handicaps of those sides were similar in composition, and strategies for exploiting advantages deriving from those handicaps tended to resemble one another.

On the political level, the status quo competitors of the

Source: From *An Outline History of China* (Peking: Foreign Language Press, 1958).

Communists were inclined, with the possible exception of the northern general Feng Yü-hsiang, to locate the majority of their stones among social, economic, and political elites and the immediate satellites and affiliates of those elites. By contrast, the political participation by the mass of the population was marginal; and organized bases of popular support for the rival factions were nonexistent.[5] In view of the hypothesized correspondence between socio-economic centrality and nearness to the center of the board, this was a wei-ch'i pattern. In the handicap positions prescribed for handicap wei-ch'i games, the handicap stones project influence for their side across the entire board, even as in republican China the elite stood in a relation of politico-military dominance to the peasant mass. Handicap men, however, are never located nearer the periphery than four lines from the edge of the board, and detailed analysis shows that even stones on the so-called 4-4 points (corner dots in Diagram 1) do not actually control potential territory along the edges.[6] The handicap is essentially a center-of-the-board structure.[7]

The political strategy of the Communists' opponents affected not only the situation prevailing on our 1927 baseline; it also foreshadowed behavior patterns of anti-Communist forces in China up to 1949. The strategy is, therefore, worth considering in more detail in its sociological context. In general, the political behavior of the non-Communist players, again with the exception of Feng Yü-hsiang, and perhaps also of his Shansi compatriot Yen Hsi-shan, may be defined as elite-oriented. Warlords, Nationalists, and local magnates competed for authority and influence over one another in an essentially closed conflict system in which the common man was seldom a significant participant.[8] In wei-ch'i terms, the handicap players were striving to consolidate influence and territory in the socio-

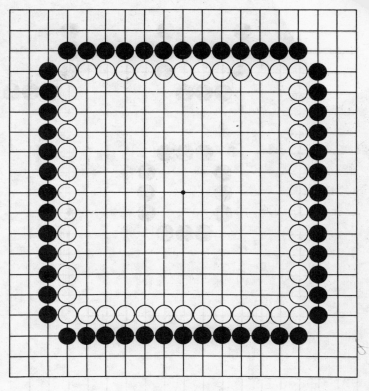

DIAGRAM 11

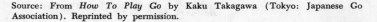

Source: From *How To Play Go* by Kaku Takagawa (Tokyo: Japanese Go Association). Reprinted by permission.

economic center of the human board. The rationale of these attempts, of the constant defections and recombinations of alliances, was plausible enough: politically and economically, the support of an influential provincial governor was worth more than that of an impoverished and undistinguished peasant. Within the framework of wei-ch'i logic, however, the preoccupation of the opponents of the Com-

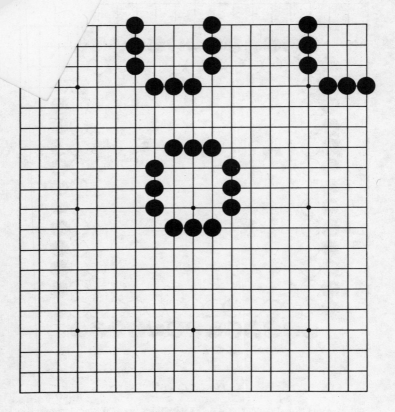

DIAGRAM 12

Source: From *How To Play Go* by Kaku Takagawa (Tokyo: Japanese Go Association). Reprinted by permission.

munists with acquiring human territory in the center of the board, while disregarding the peasant mass at its edge, was incorrect strategy for two reasons.

First, considering the inequality of distribution of wealth and power in republican China, the elite of the human board was quantitatively unimportant. The middle classes—

Mao's bourgeoisie—were likewise relatively small in number, a phenomenon common in nonindustrialized nations. Wei-ch'i is a quantitative game, in which the amount of territory controlled by a player, not the location of that territory, determines his chances of victory. The quantitative discrepancy between the number of intersections in the center and those along the sides of a wei-ch'i board may be seen from Diagram 11, in which White, who controls the center, has 121 points of territory, whereas Black, who controls the edges, has 140 (assuming, as in modern scoring procedures, that we do not count as territory those points which are occupied by stones).[9] Invariably, therefore, the first battles of a well-played wei-ch'i game center about attack and defense of the corners and sides.

Second, the center intersections of the human board of republican China shared with the center of its wei-ch'i counterpart the undesirable strategic attribute of being difficult to influence and control. Because of the prevalence of opportunism, the political loyalty of the elite and of the bourgeoisie was hard to secure and maintain. Some elementary wei-ch'i texts have a diagram (reproduced here as Diagram 12) which shows the similar instability of the wei-ch'i center. In cost/effectiveness language, it is evident that, in Diagram 12, the ratio of stones invested to territory gained in the center is 12/9; in the region along the sides, 9/9; and, in the corners, only 6/9.[10] Although this schematized analysis oversimplifies the situation, the absolute size of the region near the edge is not the only stimulus which should induce a wei-ch'i player to concentrate his territory-building along the edges of the board.

Even as the political handicaps of the anti-Communist sides were oriented toward the center of the human board, so their military counterparts, especially the elite contingents, were likewise concentrated toward the middle of the geographic board: in cities, plains, and along lines of communication. By contrast, military influence exerted by the opponents of the Communists in the outlying countryside and hinterland was more negative than positive.[11] Their principal interest in edge-of-the-board regions derived from whatever value these regions might have as sources of revenue. As long as sufficient military hegemony was exercised over the edge to insure collection of taxes, more positive types of control—garrisoning of regular troops, elimination of bandits and petty warlords, and effective policing of the district—tended to be neglected.[12] For this reason at the outset of the Communist insurgency, the future opponents of the Communists, including the Nationalists, had failed to develop the stable structure of military control and administration throughout their spheres of influence necessary to convert that influence into territory—a fact eloquently illustrated by the relative ease with which the Communists were able to carve out large territorial bases in many rural districts of China.

The strategy which prompted concentration in the center of the board of military power hostile to the Communists derived principally from the political aims and aspirations of the non-Communist players. To the warlords—and this observation applies equally to the Nationalists—political existence was a direct function of constant revenue. Revenue might be derived from taxation, or simply from loot; but in either case the more wealthy the area, the better the chances for future expansion. The most lucrative areas of China were precisely those areas which we have defined as constituting the center: the river valleys, the cities and larger towns, the rail lines, and the farming plains. In part because of this economic potential, these were the districts whose control meant prestige and concomitantly favorable bargaining positions in the chronic political maneuvering of the period.[13] In short, the military behavior was structurally identical to its political counterpart: the smallness of the area of the center of the board was of little importance compared with the political and economic value of the area.

From the wei-ch'i point of view, this rationale—comparable to that of many wei-ch'i novices who direct their play toward mapping out apparently strategic territories in the center—was incorrect for reasons similar to those which made the political objective of the opponents nonadaptive: it is difficult to form safe groups, and even harder to surround a significant amount of territory in the center of the board; and the center is quantitatively smaller in area than the edges. To rephrase these arguments in military terms: absolute control of a few key points, including cities, and of lines of communications connecting them, is tenuous and insecure when the area around those key regions—the edge of the board—is undominated and potentially hostile. Both the Japanese and the Nationalists were to discover this to their cost in operations against the Communists. Furthermore, if cities and industrial areas are specified as the center of the board, then the ratio of center to noncenter intersections was, in the China of the period under discussion, on the order of one to several hundreds.

To decide that control of these regions was an objective necessary and, for the most part, sufficient for strategic success was therefore like deciding that, in wei-ch'i, control of the center intersection constitutes victory.[14] Similarly, the decision that the so-called key economic areas of China— the Yellow River and Yangtze valleys, the West River valley in south China, and eastern Szechwan province (see Map 1)—were the significant regions of the geographic board would be equivalent to a fiat that the genuinely key territory in wei-ch'i is that formed more than six intersections from the edge.[15]

In summary, the geopolitical pattern of the Chinese board at the outset of the Communist insurgency was analogically similar to the beginning of a handicap wei-ch'i game: the center-oriented stones of the Nationalist and warlord handicap exerted influence over the entire board but firmly controlled only a small fraction of it. The strategy of the opponents which the Communists faced was distinguished by many of the same inadequacies typically found in the strategic behavior of the wei-ch'i novice: inadequacies which could be exploited by a more practiced rival. The game was ready for the appearance of the political personification of a wei-ch'i strategist.

The Chinese Communists, 1927

The Chinese Communists had, in 1927, slightly more material advantages than does White at the beginning of a handicap wei-ch'i game. Besides their party organization, decimated though it was by Nationalist purges, the Communists possessed a few small zones of political influence, principally in the peasant associations of central China, as well as a few scattered military or paramilitary forces.[16] These advantages, however, were so miniscule when set against the magnitude of Chinese Communist objectives—control of the political and military boards of China—that they do not seriously weaken the analogy between the strategic situation of the Communists and that of White at the beginning of a handicap wei-ch'i game.

The Communist leaders, moreover, lacked the decided superiority in strategico-tactical skill over their opponents which is a necessary condition for the role of White in a handicap wei-ch'i game. Whatever wei-ch'i criticisms may be raised against the ultimate strategy of the non-Communist players, their tactics were at least occasionally effective. Hence the Chinese Communists, while "struggling to keep the Red Flag flying," underwent in the early Kiangsi years considerable selective pressures to evolve effective mechanisms of insurgent action.

During this period, then, it is hardly surprising that many different and frequently contradictory solutions to various problems of revolutionary leadership were suggested by different Communist leaders. Western scholars have tried hard to determine in historical retrospect the often ambiguous interactions of these various doctrines and the personal equations which motivated them. It must be made clear, however, in this initial discussion of the Communist player, that the testing of the wei-ch'i hypothesis is independent of the political biographies of Chinese Communist decision makers. Whether or not a wei-ch'i strategy was used by insurgent forces at a given place and time is effectively decidable without reference to the specific architect of the strategy. It is, therefore, permissible to call on convenience and to label as "Maoist," directly from its 1927 beginnings, the strategic position that was ultimately to survive the Kiangsi disputes and to guide Communist party policy during the rapid rise to power during the 1940's. Certainly after 1935 it was Mao Tse-tung who was the principal articulator of the "line" we have semantically tagged with his name. It is this strategy which we shall henceforth parallel with wei-ch'i play.

THE POLITICAL PROBLEM AND ITS SOLUTION

In the preceding two sections of this chapter we have prepared the game for play: identified the players and described the board and the handicap. Now the game itself begins. We start by considering the opening political strategy of the Communist player.

In wei-ch'i, the objective of each player is to dominate with his stones as much of the board area as possible. In the Chinese Communist insurgency, the ultimate strategic goal of the insurgent side was to maximize stable control over all parts of the national human board, the Chinese people. By contrast to the political objectives characteristic of many of the non-Communist sides—and to the verbal pronouncements of some—this ultimate revolutionary purpose harmonized with the overriding territorial aim of the wei-ch'i player.[17]

In large part, the internal discord in the Chinese Communist party during the Kiangsi period derived from differences over concrete political policies to be used in implementing the territorial goal. In similar fashion, the wei-ch'i beginner perceives his objectives without definite or consistent notion of how to attain them. Theories of encirclement of political territory propounded at various times during the period were two: those which delineated the proletariat as the prime mover of the revolution; and those which substituted the peasant class in that role. This dichotomy represents, of course, an over-simplification of the issues involved; and, furthermore, these strategic doctrines are neither mutually exclusive nor collectively exhaustive. Nevertheless, since the purpose of the present analysis is not historical reconstruction but rather general interpretation aimed at deeper understanding of the Maoist theory and philosophy of revolution, the proletarian/peasant dichotomy is operationally sufficient.

As one faction, therefore, the Chinese Communist leadership included adherents of orthodox Marxist-Leninist views, supported by Comintern directives, which held that control of the proletariat was the key to success, a necessary and sufficient political condition of revolutionary victory.[18] The rationale of this doctrine, not unlike the rationale underlying the political operations of the opponents of the Communists, has several deficiencies when considered in the light of wei-ch'i theory. First, the ratio of the proletariat to the total population of China was, as of 1927, approximately 2:361.[19] To consider support by the proletariat equivalent to insurgent victory was analogous to the assumption that control of two intersections of the 19×19 wei-ch'i board is equivalent to success in a wei-ch'i game. Although the proletariat was not—by analogic measure of nearness to the edge of the board—a portion of the center of the human board, nevertheless it shared with the socio-economic center a paucity of numbers equaled by no other major class in Mao Tse-tung's 1926 stratification of Chinese society.[20]

Second, even assuming the correctness of the view that the proletariat was a potentially important, even decisive, ingredient in Chinese Communist insurgent victory, the question remains whether the Chinese Communists were, during the Kiangsi period, in a position to gain the active and organized support of that class. The proletariat lived, by definition, in cities and industrial areas: by analogic use of wei-ch'i, in the centermost regions of the center of the geographic board. As stressed above, these regions were strenuously fought for and jealously defended by the opponents of the Communist player. In order to gain a proletarian base within the regions, the Chinese Communists would have faced a situation designed to defeat their goal: the attempt of their rivals to annihilate by military means the very mass support needed for Communist success. As the Chinese Communists had learned to their discomfiture in 1927, any political stone can be captured by a military one; and military capture implies political elimination. However, even the fledgling Red Army of the Kiangsi period, as a trial battle at Changsha in 1930 proved, was in no way prepared to fight the elite military stones which would be used to suppress any important political uprisings among the urban proletariat.[21] In effect, the proletariat-oriented strategists were attempting to transfer a somewhat chesslike pattern of Western Communist strategic behavior to a revolutionary environment naturally wei-ch'i in its political ecology.[22]

It remained for the adherents of the other pole of the strategic spectrum—Mao Tse-tung, Chu Teh, and their supporters—to understand the wei-ch'i impracticality of the strategic views held by Moscow-oriented comrades. Although retaining verbally the proletariat as the vanguard of the revolution, the Maoist line emphasized Mao Tse-tung's 1927 estimate that seventy per cent of the political base of Chinese Communist power should be peasant.[23] As a matter of fact, no attempt was made to ensure that the residual thirty per cent of the social momentum be derived from proletarian origins. Hence in practice, if not in theory, the Maoist strategists rejected the proletariat as prime mover of the revolution.

The peasant-directed Maoist line was good wei-ch'i strategy for reasons which are the logical converse of those that rendered the opponents' center-oriented strategy invalid wei-ch'i technique. Numerically, the peasants shared with the wei-ch'i edge an importance denied the centers of their respective boards. In wei-ch'i the edge dominates—in the military sense of the term—the center region; in the social structure of republican China, controlling the peasants provided a secure, if subsistence-level, socio-economic base which no other class could offer. Moreover, the peasants were the most exploited and oppressed class of Chinese society; as such, they could easily be influenced to support the

Communist movement. Promised payoffs in exchange for political and military support could be both small and cheap, well within the modest power of the embryonic insurgency: land redistribution and revenge on "local gentry" constituted principal stimuli.

In practice, ease of influence was made even greater by the lack of competition afforded by the opponents of the Communists with respect to the vital social space which was the peasant class. It is a significant commentary on the strategic outlook of the many anti-Communist factions in China that no constructive and systematic program of land reform and social legislation was consistently implemented by any one of them and that the initiative was left to the Chinese Communist party. By basing their political groups along the edge of the board, the Maoist Communists were, therefore, able to avoid the anti-wei-ch'i tendency, typical of wei-ch'i beginners and of the proletariat factions in the party, toward too early direct confrontations. "Usually they try to attack every stone which the opponent places, instead of pausing to stake off territory, which must obviously be the better plan since there are more vacant points available for capture than hostile men." [24]

THE MILITARY PROBLEM AND ITS SOLUTION

In Chinese Communist insurgent doctrine, the role of military theory is most clearly understood in the framework of its political genesis and development. The function of the military strategy of the Communists, initially formulated by Chu Teh and Mao Tse-tung in the Kiangsi years, was to defend political territory and to save political stones from encirclement by the military forces of hostile sides. In order to achieve these objectives, zones of political influence had also to be made into military territories, usually termed base areas.

Because the proletariat was urban, the faction of Chinese Communist political strategists during the Kiangsi period which placed emphasis on gaining their support desired territories in and around cities, much like communes after the Paris fashion. Peasant-oriented strategists, however, naturally sought formation of countryside base areas and minimization of military operations directed against urban population centers. The resulting controversy concerning location of base areas relative to the analogic edge of the geographic board was structurally similar to, and derived from, the political dispute discussed in the preceding section. From the wei-ch'i point of view, the Maoists were correct.

The geographic center, as we have already stressed, was difficult to influence and control, perhaps even more difficult than the human center. This assertion is especially true for the opening phases of the Chinese Communist insurgency when the military forces available to the movement were, again citing the 1930 attack on Changsha, insufficient to hold even a medium-sized city for a sustained period of time. By contrast, the countryside was not normally a locus of power for either warlords or the national government, and, by the time elite troops could be concentrated against a newly emerged Communist base in the hinterland, the Communists frequently had had ample time for consolidation and acquisition of political territory. Wei-ch'i-type cost/effectiveness considerations dictated a rural strategy for the Communists.

To view the subject from another perspective: the geographic structure of the China board, like the grid-system of its wei-ch'i counterpart, frequently was such as to allow a player dominating the edge to threaten center positions. Al-

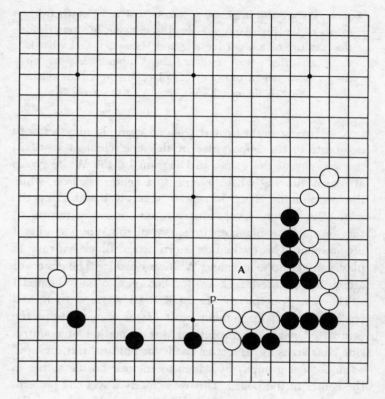

DIAGRAM 13

Source: Adapted from *Go Proverbs Illustrated* by Kensaku Segoe (Tokyo: Japanese Go Association). Reprinted by permission.

ready in the Kiangsi years, Mao Tse-tung was stressing this theme, later to be generalized as a principle of international applicability:

In northern Kiangsi we still have some basis in Tehan, Hsiushui and Tuŋgku; in western Kiangsi the Party and the Red Guards still have some strength in Ningkang, Yunghsin, Lienhua and Suichuan; in southern Kiangsi the prospects are still brighter, as the Second and Fourth Regiments of the Red Army are steadily growing in strength in the counties of Kian, Yungfeng and Hsingkuo; and what is more, the Red Army under Fang Chih-min has by no means been wiped out. All this places us in a position to close in on Nanchang [the major city of the area].[25]

A relatively sophisticated wei-ch'i example may serve to demonstrate the importance of this encirclement motif in the strategy of the game. In Diagram 13, the White group at A is occupying what amounts to a center position, while the surrounding Black forces are securely based along the edge. Our counterrevolutionary intuitions might inform us that no decisive Black encirclement of the White southeast is imminent. This evaluation is erroneous. Black has only to play a single stone at p, and White is dead.[26] (The effects of attempted counterattack are too complex to be indicated.)

The first principle of Maoist Kiangsi warfare, then, and one adhered to throughout most of the remainder of the protracted game of revolution, was formation of countryside base areas as protective shells for political territory and as stones (or groups) by which to encircle hostile stones in the center of the board. This was clearly a wei-ch'i pattern.

Another related aspect of playing near the edge of the board also deserves attention. The implication underlying the doctrine of countryside base areas is that optimal territory acquisition should be oriented toward the edge of a *natural* board. A complementary principle of Mao's military theory, also initially formulated in the Kiangsi years, was that, wherever possible, bases should be formed on the common boundary of two or more provinces, that is, along the edges of adjoining *artificial* boards.[27] (For the results of implementation of this principle as of 1933–34, see Map 3.)

The wei-ch'i justification of this further ramification of Mao Tse-tung's territorial concept lies in the deep division of the China of the 1920's and 1930's along provincial lines.[28] The strategy of the border area base minimized danger of attacks from provincial warlords or governors: the individual controlling a province upon which a Communist base adjoined often did not wish to risk play upon his neighbor's board, that is, to move troops into a bordering province. The advantage for the Communists was similar to that which would be possessed by the third player in a three-player wei-ch'i game if the other two players divided the board between them into two sub-boards with each limiting play to his own theater of operations, whereas the third player was permitted to play, and did play, upon both sub-boards. Unless concerted action—unlikely in view of Chinese political factionalism—could be achieved between the first two players, the border area territories formed by the third player would be virtually invincible: neither of his opponents could violate the other's board to complete the encirclement necessary for wei-ch'i capture.

ENCIRCLEMENT AND COUNTERENCIRCLEMENT

Although most of the wei-ch'i analysis in this chapter has focused on what might be termed macro-strategic policy problems relating to the total national situation in China, nevertheless certain smaller boards, especially those occupied by a countryside base and its environs, are also worthy of consideration. Games or sequential parts of games on these smaller boards during the Kiangsi period consisted principally of the defense of a given soviet against attack by hostile military forces. Since the attack was usually in the form of strategic encirclement, actual or attempted, and since strategic encirclement is an operation characteristic of wei-ch'i, it is not surprising that a wei-ch'i strategic defense evolved.[29]

In general, the objectives of the Communists were those of a player defending an attacked position in wei-ch'i: first, defense of the base area and preservation of the military forces protecting it—in wei-ch'i terms, maintenance of influence and protection of stones; second, the annihilation, if possible, of the attacking force in whole or in part—that is, capture of hostile stones. To these basic aims was usually joined the hope that, if a successful counteroffensive could be developed, the territory of the base area could—as often in wei-ch'i under similar circumstances—be extended, that is, territory new to the defenders could be encircled.

A brief sketch of the typical situation at the beginning of a campaign may clarify the factors involved in implementing these wei-ch'i goals. On the human level, the Communists tended to possess what Mao in 1938 was to term absolute superiority and initiative.[30] Both the army and, for the most part, the people of a Communist base area were both political stones and territory, a fact which greatly aided acquisition of the type of military intelligence claimed for the Communists in the preceding chapter. By contrast, the enemy had scant political influence, even among his own troops. The people outside the base area, if not pro-Communist, were relatively uninfluenced intersections. In short, the over-all political situation was comparable to that occurring in a three-dimensional analogic wei-ch'i game in which one player has a very large—perhaps thirteen-stone—handicap on the lower (political) level of a $19 \times 19 \times 2$ board.

On the military level, there was usually a marked difference between the capabilities of the opposing sides at the outset of a campaign. The Communist army generally had excellent mobile warfare capability: light equipment, speed on the march, stamina, and reliable intelligence about enemy strengths, activities, and intentions. However, these guerrilla warfare advantages were offset by the weak capability of the Communist forces in positional warfare, lacking as they did heavy equipment, a sufficient quantity of small arms and ammunition, and often adequate manpower. The assets and liabilities of the opposing forces, on the other hand, tended to be mirror opposites of those of the Communists. Hampered by poor morale, limited mobility, and inadequate intelligence, the Nationalist or warlord army was ill-suited to engage the flexible and disciplined Communists. However, the attackers usually had heavier and more plentiful arms than the Communists, as well as substantial numerical superiority.

As in the case of the general theories regarding politico-military bases discussed above, Communist doctrines for the destruction of strategic encirclements of base areas may be arranged on a spectrum; and this spectrum may be approximated by two general doctrines. One of these theories favored confrontations with the main enemy forces on the perimeter of, or even outside of, the base area. The other, later associated with the names of Mao Tse-tung and Chu Teh, required premeditated strategic retreat followed by encircling counterattack when conditions for such a move seemed favorable.[31]

In wei-ch'i terms, confrontation represented an attempt to defend Communist territory and influence by placing a line of stones on the periphery of the base and directly across the axis of enemy advance. Such a policy was potentially attractive in that, if it was successful, it quickly terminated the campaign, while preserving the ecological purity of the revolutionary sphere of influence. Unlike its classic naval counterpart, however, this type of "crossing the T" was operationally undesirable, given the asymmetrical positional-warfare capabilities of the players.

In wei-ch'i strategy, the terms "mobile," "light," and "economical" are sometimes used to describe distributions of stones which minimize redundant dissemination of influence and maximize the possibility of extending in various directions.[32] (Refer again to Diagram 7, in which the White collections have this mobility, but the collection of Black does not.) These terms equally describe the mobile warfare capability of the Communist army, small in size but efficient in maneuver. In wei-ch'i, when a "mobile" position of this nature is subjected to vigorous enemy attack, it is generally incorrect strategy to adopt a policy of direct containment. By prosecuting a "heavy" defense, the defender will minimize the advantages which might accrue from the "light" character of his deployments. An example may be found in the sequence presented in Diagram 14 A, of which an analyst has remarked:

> Therefore the direct contact play with Black 4 results in solidifying White's position and in a severe impairment of the efficiency of Black 2 which made the squeeze-play.[33]

In holding a doctrine in its essentials antithetic to the confrontation strategy—a theory of warfare in General André Beaufre's "indirect mode"—Mao Tse-tung and Chu Teh offered a method of achieving Communist objectives which was fully consonant with the wei-ch'i concept of rationality.[34] The strategic retreat—in military terminology, retrograde movement—upon which their defensive theory rested was a highly directed, finite, bounded operation with complex ramifications which are at once theoretical and practical. However, one fundamental wei-ch'i concept underlay the theory: retreat was a dynamic mechanism for preserving

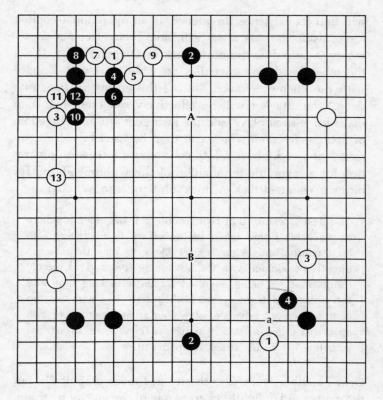

DIAGRAM 14

Source: A. Adapted from *Go Proverbs Illustrated* by Kensaku Segoe (Tokyo: Japanese Go Association). Reprinted by permission. B. Adapted from *Go Proverbs Illustrated*. Reprinted by permission.

a favorable balance of *hsien-shou*—the wei-ch'i version of strategic initiative.

If a guerrilla force is set in direct confrontation with even a comparatively primitive genre of modern military apparatus, the guerrilla commander will be forced to make constant response to his mechanically superior opponent. Eventually the pressure will become too intense and the guerrilla force will find its existence threatened as an operational combat force, while its base areas will have their efficiency as severely impaired as those of Black in Diagram 14 A. If, on the other hand, the guerrillas are able to retreat in pace with the enemy advance, "luring the enemy to penetrate deep," the attacker will be effectively rendered unable to make *hsien-shou* plays, and the insurgent will have freedom of action—freedom which can then be used to recruit, indoctrinate, and, above all, to concentrate forces in preparation for a favorable termination of the withdrawal and for ultimate counterattack. As in revolution, so in wei-ch'i:

> The next question that will trouble the beginner is where to place his stones when his adversary is advancing into his territory, and beginners are likely to play their stones directly in contact with the advancing forces. This merely results in their being engulfed by the attacking line, and the stones and territory are both lost. If you wish to stop your adversary's advance, play your stones a space or two apart from his, so that you have a chance to strengthen your line before his attack is upon you.[35]

Or, as another wei-ch'i authority has more graphically put the matter, "Play lightly in areas where the enemy is strong. If you cannot (hold your ground) in such areas, run out quickly." [36]

In Diagram 14 B, we illustrate one instance of this Maoist option: under attack by White 1 and 3, Black does not play in contact at a but rather "runs out quickly" with 4. Of this maneuver the veteran quoted above remarks:

> Here the result of using Black 4 at A [= a in Diagram 14 B] would be even worse for Black than it was in the similar situation of the preceding diagram [14 A], for it has even less effect on the attacking White stone, White 3.

> It is good play to strike diagonally upward with Black 4; this has the advantage that it *does not provoke White's consolidation in response* [emphasis supplied].[37]

In the Maoist theory of revolutionary warfare, as initially developed in the Kiangsi period, retreat is inevitably to be followed by large-scale and effective counterattack. There is some question as to how frequently this pattern occurred in early Communist warfare: especially in the Kiangsi days, it seems likely that the simple Clausewitzian law of the diminishing force of the offensive was as strong a motivating factor in eventual enemy retreat as was major Communist counteraction. Because of this consideration, and because more is known about Communist offensive operations during the 1945–49 civil war than about their Kiangsi forebearers, detailed treatment of the Maoist attack on enemy stones will be reserved for a later chapter. One theoretical point is nevertheless worth establishing in anticipation of this later development.

In the word "wei-ch'i," the morpheme "wei" signifies "encirclement." Whatever the tactics of a Communist counteroffensive of the Maoist model, the strategic principle of that counteroffensive was encirclement: the division and surrounding of enemy troops. Speaking of the first major defensive campaign waged by his forces in Kiangsi in 1930, Mao Tse-tung said:

> We had an independent division of over 1000 men in Hsingkuo some tens of li southwest of (Chang's) Lungkang. *It could encircle the enemy's rear and mass the greatest strength.* [Italics added.]

and, more generally,

> We can turn a big "encirclement and suppression campaign" waged by the enemy against us into a number of

small, separate campaigns of encirclement and suppression waged by us against the enemy.[38]

The common emphasis of Maoist military strategy and of wei-ch'i theory upon encirclement reflects the mutual homogeneity of their respective strategic psychologies. To claim that encirclement is never employed in other systems of military action, or that it does not play a role in other games, would be ridiculous. But, in these other conflict systems, encirclement is a form of strategic behavior which customarily becomes prominent only under conditions of almost absolute superiority in favor of the encircler—as, for example, in counterguerrilla warfare encirclement of a revolutionary base. In wei-ch'i, however, encirclement is part of the offensive arsenal of the attacked. The willingness of Mao, writing in the late 1930's, to ascribe a pivotal role to the encirclement motif in operations during the first years of Communist weakness would seem to indicate an early and fundamental affinity between Maoist-type warfare and wei-ch'i, "the encircling chess."

THE KIANGSI PERIOD AS A WEI-CH'I OPENING

The Kiangsi period in the Chinese Communist insurgency was similar in many of its strategic contours to a wei-ch'i opening, that is, approximately the first fifty moves of the game as played on the 19 × 19 board. The insurgency boards, political and military, were vast in comparison to the strategic forces available to any single player in 1927: the opening strategic position partook of the fluidity characteristic of the beginning of a wei-ch'i game. The strategic decisions made by the Communists were similar in content to those which a wei-ch'i player must make at the outset of the contest: which were the most important regions of the board to be controlled, and what basic operational strategy was to be followed in implementation of the objectives. The strategic problems which the Communists faced were akin to those confronted by a player without a handicap in a handicap version of the game: how to infiltrate enemy spheres of influence and set up secure bases, at the same time defending those bases against vigorous counterattacks.

In many respects—and in this a possible divergence from wei-ch'i played on the conventional board may be noted—the Communist player was not significantly stronger in 1935, at the end of the Long March, than in 1927 or 1928. Materially, he had lost before or during the Long March almost all that had previously been gained: stones, territory, influence. Detailed description of strategic blunders on the part of the Communist high command, doctrinally disunited at least through 1935—blunders which led to the fall of the central soviet base in Kiangsi and to numerous other setbacks—could only lead to repetition of the wei-ch'i analyses of previous sections. Material losses and strategic errors did not, however, prove decisive. It must be remembered that the wei-ch'i opening played by the Communists during those Kiangsi years was infinitely more complex and extensive than an opening played on a wei-ch'i board of any size. If loss of one corner, or one battle, on the conventional game-grid is not necessarily decisive to the strategic outcome of a wei-ch'i game, how much less decisive were the initial Communist misplays and setbacks in the game of insurgency played between the Communists and their opponents.

An essay in *Selected Military Works* dated soon after the Long March comments on the inapplicability to Maoist revolution of a proverb connected with another Chinese chess, hsiang-ch'i: "One careless move loses the whole game." This proposition, says the text in paraphrase, can refer only to a move effecting the situation as a whole, a move decisive for the total situation. It cannot refer to a move of partial nature, a move not in itself decisive.[39]

As events proved, the Long March which marked the end of the Kiangsi period for the Communists was by no means the last move in their insurgent game.

FOUR

THE SINO-JAPANESE WAR

In 1927 the most pertinent general observation which could have been made about the wei-ch'i game of Chinese politics concerned the number and diversity of its participants: Communist, Nationalist, and warlord. As we move into the late 1930's, the diversity of players remains, but number and fragmentation have substantially decreased. Starting with 1937 as a new baseline for comparison, we may effectively approximate the Chinese political situation by a three-person wei-ch'i game. One player was Nationalist; another, Communist; and a third, Japanese (at least from the outbreak of the Sino-Japanese conflict in 1937). Each of the three sides possessed a considerable degree of centralization in policy decision-making. Although the precise political roles of Mao Tse-tung and his personal adherents remained unclear for several years from 1935 into the early 1940's, there is little doubt that, after 1935, Mao was the main expositor of the Chinese Communist strategic position.

Before beginning systematic wei-ch'i analysis of Chinese Communist strategy in the 1937–45 period, a description of the historical background may serve to provide continuity. In 1935, the fortunes of the Communists were at a low ebb. To what extent failure was due to deviation from correct wei-ch'i play is, in retrospect, largely undecidable.[1] In any case, in October 1934 the Communists took the characteristic wei-ch'i step of abandoning a dead position in one corner of the board with the objective of playing elsewhere to greater advantage. After a year of retreat across the far-western reaches of China, under constant harassment by anti-Communist military forces and by hostile tribesmen, the survivors of the Long March joined forces in Shensi with indigenous Communist partisan units which had been operating in that area since 1927. The wei-ch'i groups thus connected were able, in combination, to defend an almost literal edge-of-the-board position against repeated Nationalist offensives. Bounded on the north and east by the upper course of the Yellow River, the Shensi soviets were corner bases on the board of China proper. In a political sense, too, Shensi was a border area: in the 1930's, as for years before, the areas of Sinkiang and Inner Mongolia were only peripherally influenced by any Chinese government, thus making effective Nationalist geopolitical encirclement of the Communist strongholds an impossibility. "If you have lost four corners, resign," says a well-known wei-ch'i proverb.[2] The Yenan area of Shensi province was a corner saved from the general Communist defeat of 1935 and, as such, not only permitted the Communists to remain in the game but also proved a crucial factor in their expansion after 1937.

When the Japanese took advantage of the Marco Polo bridge incident in July 1937 to initiate a large-scale land invasion of the Chinese mainland, an exogenous factor transformed the political and strategic situation. Rapidly overwhelming Chinese resistance in Shanghai and at various points in north China, the Japanese army advanced along Chinese railway lines, capturing city after city. Taiyuan, the major city of Shansi province, fell in November 1937; it was followed by Nanking and Hankow. Principally for logistical reasons, however, the tempo of advance could not be maintained. As we now know, Japanese strategy in Asia called for only limited military investment in the China theater. In the winter of 1938 and spring of 1939, the Japanese controlled many of the central economic and population districts of China: the lower Yangtze valley and the Yellow River region to the north. The military situation stabilized along a front which was to constitute the extent of Japanese penetration for the duration of the war, with the exception of one additional major drive into southwest China in 1944 (see Map 4 for an approximate indication of the position).[3]

This relatively rapid stabilization following initial blitzkrieg was the determinant governing the interactions of the three players identified above. Out of this triad, three two-player games could logically develop. One of these— Nationalist-Japanese—quickly became, with the tacit agreement of both parties, relatively latent. A second— Nationalist-Communist—was legally terminated in September 1937 by formation of a nominal united front of both parties for the duration of the struggle with Japan. In reality, hostilities were to resume sporadically for the remainder of the war. However, omission of this unimportant game from our wei-ch'i reasoning will not upset analysis of the central principles of Chinese Communist insurgent strategy.

JAPAN IN CHINA
Main area of penetration, about 1940

U. S. S. R.

Amur R.

HEILUNGKIANG

MONGOLIA

MANCHUKUO

KIRIN

CHAHAR

JEHOL

LIAONING

SUIYUAN

Peking
(Peiping)

KOREA

NINGHSIA

Paotow

HOPEI

K
A
N
S
U

SHANSI

Yellow R.

SHANTUNG

TSINGHAI

Yenan

Lanchow

SHENSI

HONAN

KIANGSU

HUPEH

Nanking

Shanghai

Hankow

ANHWEI

SZECHWAN

Ichang

Chungking

Yangtze R.

CHEKIANG

Changsha

KIANGSI

HUNAN

FUKIEN

SIKANG

KWEICHOW

YUNNAN

KWANGSI

West R.

Amoy

TAIWAN
(FORMOSA)

BURMA

Mekong R.

Canton

KWANGTUNG

Hong Kong (Br.)

FRENCH
INDOCHINA

HAINAN

0   Miles   500

THAILAND

MAP 4

This calculus was focused on the third of the three games referred to above: that between the Japanese and the Communists (behind the thick black line of Map 4) in north and eastern China. The primary target of the Communist high command was to exploit favorable conditions for developing guerrilla warfare throughout this area, warfare which was ultimately to fashion the power base from which the Communists were to defeat their Nationalist enemy in the post-1945 showdown. Beginning in a mountainous region in eastern Shansi, an extension from the corner base at Yenan, the Communists established zones of control, "liberated areas," with such success that by 1945, when Japan surrendered, about one-fifth of the population—approximately one hundred million persons—was under Communist authority. During the Sino-Japanese war period, therefore, the crucial development of Chinese Communism was largely limited to the board of the Japanese-occupied areas.[4] We now turn to consideration of wei-ch'i patterns on this board.

CHINA, 1937: STRATEGY AND GEOPOLITICS IN THE OCCUPIED AREAS

From the wei-ch'i point of view, the strategic situation in 1937 in north-central China after the Japanese conquest had exhausted its initial impetus was considerably more favorable to the Chinese Communists than at any time during the ten years previous.

On the political board, the Japanese were in a far less favorable position than their Nationalist predecessors. Despite a scattering of Chinese collaborators, the populace was hostile to the Japanese invaders, who, by their behavior, did little to change this attitude. A contemporary account has synthesized the situation well:

> There is no doubt that Japanese rule in the occupied areas
> depends in the main on coercion; there is no social basis
> for the puppet régime, and only half-hearted attempts to
> create one. . . . The peasantry was the only group large
> enough to make a social basis for Japanese rule. The
> method of dealing with the peasants, briefly speaking, has
> been one of terrorism.[5]

In a sense, therefore, the Japanese soon came to possess a
large amount of *negative* territory on the political level, that
is, in the human intersections which would voluntarily become the territory and influence of any Chinese political
force willing to enlist their support against the invader.
Even more significant quantitatively were large segments of
the rural population of north China whom the Japanese invasion and Nationalist collapse had deprived of political
leadership above the village level, and who, in effect, constituted an empty wei-ch'i board for Communist political or-
ganizers.

On the geographic level, the process of the Japanese invasion was capture of the stones of one player—the Nationalists—by those of another—the invading army. However,
because the Japanese limited themselves for the most part
to play on such center-of-the-board intersections as railways
and cities, they exercised significantly less military control
over the rural areas than had the most center-oriented of
their Chinese counterparts.[6] To quote again from the source
just cited:

> The first task in relation to the railways of North China
> was one of control [by the Japanese] rather than of devel-
> opment. Immediate steps were taken to fortify the main
> lines; certain sections, such as that from Paotingfu to
> Tinghsien, were studded with pillboxes, each capable of
> holding twenty men, about every third of a mile.[7]

And again:

> The general picture for the first year of the Provisional
> [Communist guerrilla] Government, therefore, is one of
> Japanese garrisons in all important cities along the rail-
> ways and at all bridges, small stations, and even road cross-
> ings. Garrisons, which varied all the way from twenty to
> two thousand men, were occasionally placed in cities at
> some distance from the railways, but these were not always
> permanent.[8]

In short, once more we have a pattern which was un-
adaptive from the wei-ch'i standpoint, for essentially the
same reasons spelled out in detail in the previous chapter.[9]
The philosophy underlying Japanese strategy is, as it
were, reflected in the words of one theorist of Western
chess: "Strategically, the central hub of the chessboard is
the most important part. The control of the center, therefore, is the first principle of middle-game strategy." [10] In
view of their national involvement with go (wei-ch'i), this
approach on the part of the Japanese seems paradoxical.
Perhaps, however, they viewed China as a corner of the
larger board of East Asia and the Pacific toward which their
main strategy was directed, and one which could be ignored
once their basic stones were played. Whatever the reason,
the Japanese army, considered as a set of stones, disseminated far less influence in the occupied areas than had the
Nationalists before them: certain qualitative superiorities
did not, as Mao Tse-tung perceived, compensate for quantitative inferiority. To remedy the quantitative weakness of
their forces, the Japanese commanders created puppet Chinese armies, often composed of erstwhile Nationalist units:
but the human components of these military stones were

definitely not the political territory of the Japanese and hence were often ineffective militarily.

THE CHINESE COMMUNISTS, 1937

During the Sino-Japanese war, because of the united front agreed to by the Communists and the Nationalists, the strategic boards of the Communist player were effectively limited to the geographic extent and the population of the Japanese-occupied areas. The objectives of the Communists in this somewhat restricted portion of China proper were the same as those set forth by Mao Tse-tung and his associates during the Kiangsi period. In accordance with Mao's theory of revolutionary strategy, the primary Communist military objective was formation of territory: creation of territorial bases or liberated areas behind Japanese lines. That the Chinese Communists recognized the similarity of this target with wei-ch'i procedure is indicated by statements (quoted in the Introduction) in Mao's *Selected Military Works*.[11] The secondary military objective was capture of hostile stones where possible: annihilation of Japanese and puppet forces. Given the qualitative strength of Japanese forces and their relative concentration, the degree to which the Communist player was able to implement achievement of this secondary objective was often marginal. A similar state of affairs frequently prevails in wei-ch'i: the rate of capture is often very low, and that fraction of a player's final score which derives from territory often exceeds by a factor of ten times that contributed by capture.

On the political level, the primary goal of the Communists was also formation of territory: broadening and consolidation of active and organized popular support among the rural masses. The corresponding negative objective was elimination, by intimidation or persuasion, of Chinese who collaborated either with the invader or with any other anti-Communist political element: that is, the capture of hostile political stones. In addition, also as a negative objective on the political level, the Communists attempted to win the support of—to capture politically—Japanese army person-nel, and especially the sympathies of those Japanese whom they held as prisoners. One of the three political principles for military action defined in Mao Tse-tung's *On Protracted War* (1938) is "disintegration of the enemy forces." Said Mao:

> To apply these principles effectively, we must start with this basic attitude . . . of respect for the human dignity of prisoners of war once they have laid down their arms. Those who take all this as a technical matter and not one of basic attitude are indeed wrong, and they should correct their view.[12]

Although no spectacular success was gained by application of propaganda methods during the war with Japan, the ex-perience gained by the Communists in that laboratory was to prove invaluable in large-scale capture by political means of Nationalist military groups in the 1945–49 civil war in China.

Such, in brief, is the wei-ch'i formulation of the strategic objectives of the Communist movement in the occupied areas. The operational problem of the Communists during the Sino-Japanese war was not determination of strategic aims—Mao had already fixed these in early phases of the game—but codification and systematization of the strategic techniques used to attain these objectives. It was imperative for the Communists to discover and implement the most efficient methods of winning the support of the entire popu-lation of the occupied areas. On the geographic level, it was necessary to develop effective military techniques for gaining control of the countryside and for forming base areas as extensions from the Yenan corner base. In wei-ch'i terms, the Communists had to develop methods of realizing in practice the encirclement of territorial regions determined by the correct edge-of-the-board orientation of their strategic goals.

WEI-CH'I ENCIRCLEMENT AND POLITICAL TERRITORY

Similarity of ends cannot always be used to infer similarity of means. Given the wei-ch'i aims of wartime Chinese Communism, however, it is only logical that the pattern of political operations developed by the Communists during the Sino-Japanese war should have paralleled the methods used in wei-ch'i to gain territory. For analytic convenience, this acquisition of psycho-political territory may, as in the task of surrounding intersections in pure wei-ch'i, be divided into two functionally different strategic phases.[13]

The first stage consisted, in effect, of gaining a political foothold in areas previously uninfiltrated. The constellation of strategic problems which here confronted Communist strategists was that of the wei-ch'i player intent on developing territorial control of comparatively vacant areas. Usually the initial step was dependent upon entrance into the target area of what may be termed "regular" stones, that is, political agitators organizationally affiliated with core elements of the Communist movement: hard-line cadres and party members, frequently sent from Yenan or from some major Communist base previously established. The propaganda and mobilization contingents attached to all regular Red Army, and to many guerrilla, units served to initiate and develop mass support, and some form of anti-Japanese local government was soon established.[14] In its central themes of economy of input and decentralization of effort, this pattern of Communist expansion was the wei-ch'i strategy of extension with dispersed forces characteristic of the territorial aspect of the game.[15] "Despite the size that some mass associations achieved, organization actually began on a very small scale." [16]

The underlying dynamic of Communist mobilization technique was encirclement, in direct analogy with that key wei-ch'i process. This encirclement was not the simple, symmetrical surrounding of a hostile force which the term has come to mean in Western strategic parlance. It was psychological encirclement: diffusion throughout the population of Communist activists who exposed their compatriots to propaganda by every conceivable means and in every conceivable quarter, exhorting, cajoling, organizing:

. . . how should we mobilize them? By word of mouth, by leaflets and bulletins, by newspapers, books and pamphlets, through plays and films, through schools, through the mass organizations and through our cadres.[17]

The objective of psychological encirclement was total: at no time and in no place should the people be free from encirclement by anti-Japanese and/or pro-Communist psychological stimuli. On developing this social environment for political ends Mao commented:

. . . to mobilize once is not enough, and political mobilization for the War of Resistance must be continuous. Our job is not to recite our political programme mechanically to the people, for nobody will listen to such recitations; we must link the political mobilization for the war with developments in the war and with the life of the soldiers and

the people, and make it a continuous movement. This is a
matter of immense importance on which our victory in the
war primarily depends.[18]

In short, the individual was the intersection; the stones were
the cadres; and propaganda devices, the tangible counterparts of the intangible weight of wei-ch'i influence which
transforms impartial intersections into the partisan territory
of one side or the other. Stability of Chinese Communist
political power during the decade after 1949 rested largely
upon nationwide application of these sophisticated wei-ch'i
techniques of psychological encirclement initially developed
during the Sino-Japanese war.[19]

Whereas the characteristic of the first phase of psycho-
political operations was expansion, that of the second may
be labeled consolidation: the filling in of encirclement patterns, the wei-ch'i analogue of which would be similar to the
transition between Diagrams 15 A and 15 B. These diagram
positions were derived from two successive time points in an
actual game by deleting obfuscating White forces in order
to illustrate with maximum clarity the evolution of Black
control. (Compare with Maps 5A and 5B, which illustrate
Japanese Army estimates of the distribution of county gov-
ernments in north China politically affiliated with the Communists in January 1938 [5A] and August 1939 [5B].) [20]

More protracted than the first phase, the second stage,
like the first, was dominated by wei-ch'i motifs. Even as wei-
ch'i stones in a hostile sphere of influence, political intransi-
gents were identified and isolated. Desirous of avoiding the
strategic disadvantages which would result from policies of
force in dealing with core anti-Communist elements, the
Chinese Communists based their behavior on the wei-ch'i
principle that to neutralize (to kill in the wei-ch'i sense)
is better than to capture. In confronting die-hards, to para-

THE GUERRILLA MOVEMENT IN NORTH CHINA

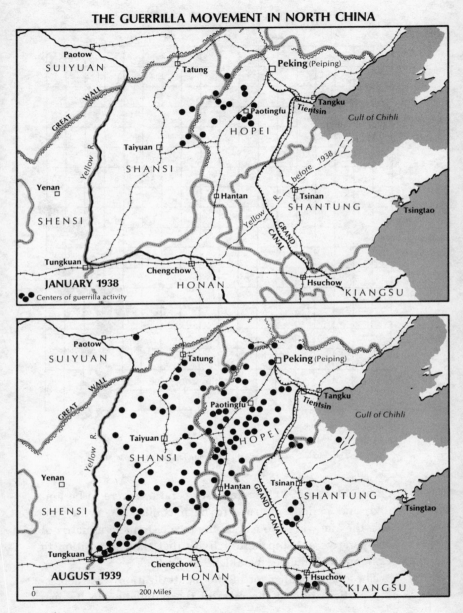

MAPS 5A AND 5B

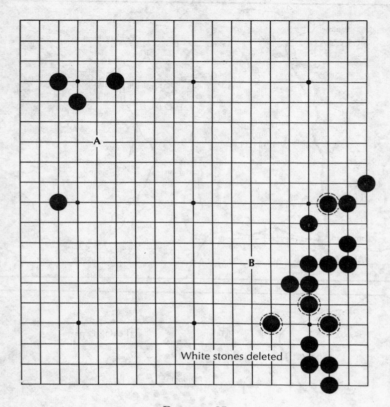

A

B

White stones deleted

DIAGRAM 15

The circled stones in B are homologues of those in A.

phrase Mao in 1940, Communist operations were to be limited, and periods of truce to be maximized.[21] As in wei-ch'i, the aim was so to embed the recalcitrants in a matrix of co-operative anti-Japanese activity that their opposition to Communist influence would be ineffectual.

The operational pivot of this neutralization was increasing participation of the mass of the population in its own

encirclement. In wei-cl
ently formulated, the m
ment, the fewer *vacant*
lower his realized score. T
trast, played a political vers1
ch'i in which stones count as
intersections: the ultimate 1
every individual simultaneous]
tory, filling at once an active a

In a broader context, the Chi
united front action aimed agains\   .as
a strategy of territorial consolit   .vn wei-ch'i
themes. Perhaps the most importa   ..evelopment in post-
1937 Maoist theory, the united front represented a shift in
Communist party policy from the Kiangsi agrarian program
based on land reform, which appealed to a restricted social
stratum, to a far more broadly conceived social stategy
founded on the Chinese nationalistic instinct to unite
against the Japanese.[23] Divesting the strategy of jargon and
tactics, we may characterize the united front policies of the
Communist player as attempts to develop support for the
Communist movement among the more conservative—because more prosperous—forces shaping Chinese society: the
more affluent peasants, the landholders, the intellectuals, the
commercial classes. In wei-ch'i terms, the doctrine of the
united front constituted a moving out toward the center of
the social board by a player who already possessed the key
to the loyalty of its periphery.

This wei-ch'i principle of movement toward the center is
essential to competent play. Reflected in the initial quotation in Chapter III (p. 52), it represents the realization that
often in wei-ch'i the externally contained edge position is
dead, *provided* that the containment is securely based on
the edge positions of the containing side.[24] Although, in

more than three or four lines from the
rable terrain, terrain they are and, as such,
ally be infiltrated. As Mao Tse-tung foresaw,
hope for Communist victory lay in *hsien-shou,* in
sure upon the opponent to make continuous response to
Communist moves. Politically, a crucial means of maintaining *hsien-shou* lay in calculated advance toward the center of the board in the early middle game, depriving the opponent (ultimately, as it turned out, the Chinese Nationalists) of any inviolate social base, no matter how centralized by our distance-from-the-edge measure. If Mao has played revolutionary wei-ch'i, it has not been the conservative, defensive wei-ch'i of pre-modern tradition but the aggressive wei-ch'i of the twentieth century.[25]

WEI-CH'I THEORY AND GUERRILLA PRACTICE

It is a safe conjecture that no other branch or category of war or violent conflict has given rise to as much poetry and metaphor as have guerrilla operations: a floating vapor, a strangling net, a muddy morass—to all these and many other natural or human phenomena has guerrilla warfare been likened. Yet guerrilla warfare remains one of the most simple, the most basic, and the most primitive manifestations of military endeavor.

The principal danger involved in indiscriminate employment of the guerrilla warfare label is the diversity of military systems which it has, in the past, been used to denote. Too frequently training suitable for the American frontier of the mid-nineteenth century has been given to American Special Forces officers sent to confront Maoist strategy in Vietnam or Thailand. One contribution of the wei-ch'i perspective may be to throw into relief the Chinese Communist insurgent model as an entire system of revolutionary action which transcends those tactical military aspects of Maoist behavior which have so fascinated Western army officers and military observers. Wei-ch'i reflects the totality of Chinese Communist strategic psychology, not merely its ill-defined guerrilla dimension.

With this caveat in mind, we may turn to the so-called guerrilla warfare of the Chinese Communists behind Japanese lines and to an assessment of its wei-ch'i structure. Once again, we may divide the development of Communist territorial control into two phases, which are the military counterparts of the political stages analyzed in the previous section.

First, from surrounding areas the Communists would introduce sufficient military force to gain some measure of military hegemony over the territory of a desired new base area. In this way, the Eighth Route Army moved across rural north China, setting up anti-Japanese bases as it progressed. Because Japanese control was nonexistent in most of the Chinese countryside, no complex military problems were customarily involved in this initial occupation; the pattern was that of Black play in Diagram 15 A, with emphasis on small-unit, dispersed operations to maximize territorial coverage and acquisition of political territory.

A second phase of encirclement occurred when, after sufficient social mobilization (that is, playing of stones on the human board), routine control could in great part be relinquished to a large number of local military and paramilitary units formed and manned by the population of the district. The militia, the "People's Self-Defense Corps" and related organizations, implemented the wei-ch'i concept of territorial defense by saturation with protective stones deployed not merely on the periphery but throughout the entire region.

> During the Communist move toward power in China . . .
> the type of strategic force applied by the insurgents, in
> contrast to that conventionally applied in land warfare in
> the West, embraced two dimensions. . . . When the Com-
> munists controlled a region, it was because they possessed,
> dispersed over the area, a large number of small units
> which coalesced on the strategic level to form a single
> force. . . .[26]

During the phase of intensification of the encirclement,
Communist operations were also directed in part against the
enemy. Post-1949 propaganda would have us believe that
large numbers of Japanese troops were annihilated by the
forces of the liberated areas. In fact, because capture and
retention of Japanese strongpoints were customarily impractical, given the certainty of overpowering counteraction, Communist policy was, once again, that of wei-ch'i
"killing." Immured in concrete pillboxes, Japanese Army
units were immobilized by constant harassment and fear of
ambush while on patrol.[27] In many instances, immobilization ultimately reached a point where Japanese positions
resembled those of dead wei-ch'i groups. "Sitting the enemy
to death" is no less a wei-ch'i technique than a Chinese
Communist method.

Various terms have been used by Mao Tse-tung to describe different degrees of Communist and Japanese control
of given regions of the north China board during the Sino-
Japanese war.[28] This classification may be profitably exam-
ined with wei-ch'i logic. *Base areas* were defined by Mao as
relatively permanent Communist strongholds, protected by
units of the Communist regular army as well as by the force
in depth outlined above, and administered by a formal governmental structure. Of course, these regions were not
actual territory in the wei-ch'i sense and with the wei-ch'i
degree of rigor. But, because they were generally invulner-

able to assault by all but a decisively strong force of Japanese, they must be designated potential territory: board areas whose ultimate transformation into territory is likely but not certain. (In fact, most of these regions remained securely under the control of the Communists until their nationwide victory in 1949.) *Guerrilla zones,* as defined by Mao, were regions which were often under Communist control but which nevertheless oscillated between the Communists and the invader. Such zones might be compared to spheres of influence in wei-ch'i. Finally, Mao also recognized *Japanese strongholds,* generally regions in the center of the geographic board. These areas may be interpreted in two ways. First, they may be seen as merely *stones* (or intersections occupied by stones) which, as in pure wei-ch'i, are vulnerable to capture unless supported by a broad base of empty territory. These regions were operational bases for the Japanese during the war, and their abandonment by the Japanese at its termination may be viewed as capture. A second alternative is to liken the Japanese strongholds to territory in the wei-ch'i sense, but to impose a discontinuity on the model and to visualize their removal in 1945 as the removal of stones at the end of *one* of the various games in progress on the China board.

Turning from the subject of operations on the geographic board, it may be relevant to sketch from the wei-ch'i viewpoint certain guerrilla tactics which made possible the concrete implementation of those operations. The wei-ch'i model is, of course, at base a strategic one and has limited relevance in the sphere of military tactics. Nevertheless, tactics and strategy are interrelated systems of military action, and certain of the strategic wei-ch'i policy of the Chinese Communists carried over into their tactical devices.

Three basic guerrilla tactics were stressed by Chinese

Communist training manuals of the period: ambush; raid; and sabotage.[29] To be sure, these methods are hardly original to the Maoist system; but that they were considered by Chinese Communist military officers to be consistent with and even inherent in that system is significant and worthy of wei-ch'i analysis. The *ambush* was defined as attack by concealed guerrilla units on a moving enemy force; the *raid*, by contrast, was a surprise strike at a static enemy unit, frequently a pillbox or other fortification. In both cases, Chinese Communist tactics emphasized encirclement on two planes: physical, leaving the enemy no avenue of escape; and psychological, exploiting the confusion and panic deriving from physical encirclement combined with effective initial surprise.[30] Both methods, therefore, were analogous to wei-ch'i motifs of encirclement of hostile stones: what is important in wei-ch'i because of that game's rule structure proved vital to guerrilla warfare on considerations of efficiency alone.

As for *sabotage*, its function was the tactical—and sometimes strategic—disconnection of enemy forces, whether of commander from army, or army from supply base, or unit U_1 from unit U_2, in respect to both transportation and communication: to quote a list from a Red Army training manual of the period, "destruction of wires and poles; of bridges, concrete and iron; of roads and railroads; of vehicles; of railroad stations; of logistic centers." [31] Such tactics may be likened to wei-ch'i isolation and separation of hostile forces, frequently a prelude to more positive and complete encirclement. In wei-ch'i and in Maoist warfare, the execution of such disconnecting maneuvers is basic to implementation of the underlying tactical concept of operations; in some future study, their wei-ch'i analysis may, by extension, serve to furnish new strategic insights.

A War of Jigsaw Pattern

Nowhere in the analysis of the Chinese Communist insurgency is the wei-ch'i analogue more pointed than in the resemblance to the middle game of the politico-military pattern of Communist base areas during the Sino-Japanese war.[32] These areas were interspersed with Japanese strongholds in north-central China in much the way that groups of opposing sides are interrelated in the wei-ch'i middle game. In the words of Mao Tse-tung:

> Thus it can be seen that the protracted and far-flung War of Resistance Against Japan is a war of jig-saw pattern militarily, politically, economically and culturally. . . . Every Chinese should consciously throw himself into this war of a jig-saw pattern. . . .[33]

A comparison of the pattern in Diagram 16 with that of Map 6 illustrates the resemblance between wei-ch'i and the situation which Mao described. In Chapter I, we described jigsaw pattern in abstract formal terms; we now proceed to develop the concept in detail. In Diagram 16 we have a typical early middle-game situation on a 19×19 board; Map 6 shows the relative deployments of Japanese and guerrillas in about 1941.[34] In both cases, White groups and territories partially surround those of Black; similarly, those of Black half-surround White's base areas. To quote Mao Tse-tung again:

> Taking the war as a whole, there is no doubt that we are strategically encircled by the enemy, because he is on the strategic offensive and operating on exterior lines, while we are on the strategic defensive and operating on interior lines. This is the first form of enemy encirclement. We on

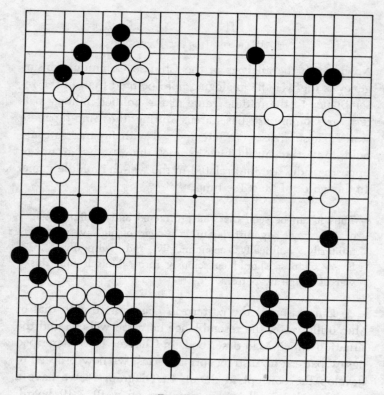

DIAGRAM 16

Source: From *Go and Go-moku* by Edward Lasker (New York: Dover Publications, Inc., 1960). Reprinted by permission of the publisher.

our part can encircle one or more of the enemy columns advancing on us along separate routes, because we apply the policy of fighting campaigns and battles from tactically exterior lines . . . This is the first form of our counter-encirclement of the enemy. Next, if we consider the guerrilla base areas in the enemy's rear, each area taken singly is surrounded by the enemy on all sides, like the Wutai mountain area, or on three sides, like the northwestern

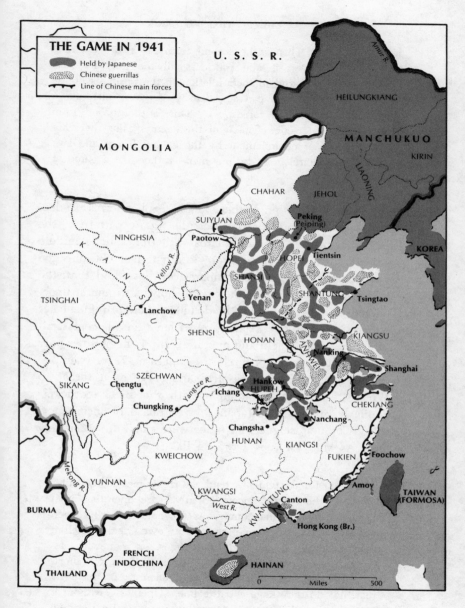

The Game in 1941

- Held by Japanese
- Chinese guerrillas
- Line of Chinese main forces

U. S. S. R.

MONGOLIA

HEILUNGKIANG

MANCHUKUO

KIRIN

LIAONING

JEHOL

CHAHAR

SUIYUAN

Peking (Peiping)

KANSU

NINGHSIA

Paotow

Yellow R.

HOPEI

Tientsin

KOREA

SHANSI

SHANTUNG

Tsingtao

TSINGHAI

Lanchow

Yenan

SHENSI

HONAN

KIANGSU

ANHWEI

Nanking

Shanghai

SZECHWAN

Chengtu

Yangtze R.

Ichang

HUPEH

Hankow

CHEKIANG

Chungking

Nanchang

SIKANG

Changsha

HUNAN

KIANGSI

FUKIEN

Foochow

KWEICHOW

Mekong R.

YUNNAN

KWANGSI

West R.

KWANGTUNG

Canton

Amoy

TAIWAN (FORMOSA)

Hong Kong (Br.)

BURMA

FRENCH INDOCHINA

THAILAND

HAINAN

0   Miles   500

MAP 6

Source: Adapted from *An Atlas of Far Eastern Politics* by G. F. Hudson, Marthe Rajchman, and G. E. Taylor. Copyright © 1942 by the Secretariat, Institute of Pacific Relations. Reprinted by permission of The John Day Company, Inc.

Shansi area. This is the second form of enemy encirclement. However, if one considers all the guerrilla base
areas together and in their relation to the positions of the
regular forces, one can see that we in turn surround a
great many enemy forces. . . . This is the second form
of our counter-encirclement of the enemy. Thus there are
two forms of encirclement by the enemy forces and two
forms of encirclement by our own—rather like a game of
weichi.[35]

For these remarks no further wei-ch'i explication is needed.
A second characteristic which the jigsaw pattern of the
1937–45 guerrilla warfare shares with the wei-ch'i middle
game is the fluidity of the strategic situation. To be sure, the
wei-ch'i middle game is comparatively less fluid than the
opening. Many areas of the board, however, remain unoc-
cupied and are not within the definite sphere of influence of
either side. Moreover, some groups have no adjacent territories to support them and operate behind enemy lines only
as elements in a larger circle. In Diagram 17, for example,
the circled stones are baseless and serve as a threat to
White's center in conjunction with the Black corners.[36]
Similarly, in the Sino-Japanese war phase of insurgency,
many Communist guerrilla bases were small and relatively
fluid. As Mao Tse-tung wrote in 1938:

The main forces, which extend the front lines to the outer
limits of the enemy's occupied areas, are operating from
the rear area of the country as a whole. . . . But each
guerrilla area has a small rear of its own, upon which it
relies to establish its fluid battle lines. . . . guerrilla de-
tachments . . . dispatched by a guerrilla area for short-
term operations in the rear of the enemy . . . have no
rear, nor do they have a battle line. "Operating without a
rear" is a special feature of revolutionary war in the new
era, wherever a vast territory . . . [is] to be found.[37]

106

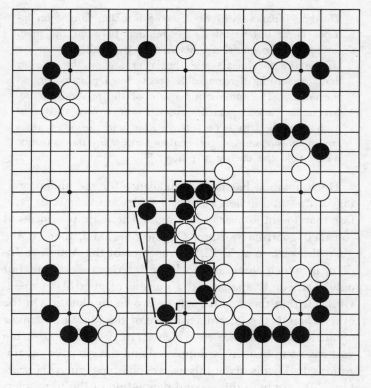

DIAGRAM 17

Source: Adapted from *Go Proverbs Illustrated* by Kensaku Segoe (Tokyo: Japanese Go Association). Reprinted by permission.

We can but re-emphasize an earlier proposition regarding the identical fluidity of wei-ch'i deployments: "A wei-ch'i player cannot assume the existence of a secure front line or a safe rear area."

Still another manifestation of jigsaw pattern common to both Maoist insurgency and wei-ch'i, and particularly evident during the 1937–45 period, is the complex system of interior and exterior lines. The distinguishing characteristics of this system have been well described by Mao Tse-tung:

The anti-Japanese war as a whole is being fought on interior lines; but as far as the relation between the main forces and the guerrilla units is concerned, the former are on the interior lines while the latter are on the exterior lines, presenting a remarkable spectacle of pincers around the enemy. The same can be said of the relationship between the various guerrilla areas. From its own viewpoint each guerrilla area is on interior lines and the other areas are on exterior lines; together they form many battle fronts, which hold the enemy in pincers.[38]

This quotation has more significance for the understanding of the total action system of Chinese Communist warfare than might appear at first sight. There are two forms of so-called guerrilla warfare. On the one hand, there is the guerrilla warfare of T. E. Lawrence or of the American Indian, in which there are no lines, interior or exterior, but only vast, empty spaces and a nucleus of guerrillas maneuvering within them as though in Brownian motion. On the other, there is the guerrilla warfare of the Maoist system or of analogous doctrines in which strategy presupposes the vast spaces to be heavily populated and the guerrilla organizations to be massive: this is wei-ch'i-type guerrilla warfare.[39] It is only in this second denotation of the term guerrilla warfare that we have the interior and exterior lines, that organized multitude of bases and stones which Mao was describing. The distinction is critical, and unconventional warfare theory may gain in clarity as the difference is recognized and appreciated.

A concrete example of the principle of interlocking lines, interior and exterior, may prove relevant. Although the Communist player formed his most powerful and extensive bases along the edges of the geographic board, in the mountainous areas of north China, he also created smaller and less stable collections on the north China plain and in the

Yangtze basin. The rationale of this policy was that, to every interior line position, there must be a corresponding exterior line position if encirclement is to be effectively developed; and that the initiative can never be gained if all effort is concentrated on the interior line in regions of comparative security. A strong wei-ch'i player, it must be remembered, especially one of the modern school, seeks not only to gain territory in the corners and along the sides but also to gain influence toward the center. The Chinese bases on the plains were like exterior-line collections such as those in Diagram 17: unconsolidated but strategically pivotal. In connection with this point of doctrine, Mao has said:

> Of course, the plains are less suitable than the mountains, but it is by no means impossible to develop guerrilla warfare or establish base areas of a sort there. The widespread guerrilla warfare in the plains of Hopei and of northern and northwestern Shantung proves that it is possible to develop guerrilla warfare in the plains. . . . It is definitely possible to conduct seasonal guerrilla warfare by taking advantage of the "green curtain" of tall crops in summer and of the frozen rivers in winter. As the enemy has no strength to spare at present and will never be able to attend to everything even when he has the strength, it is absolutely necessary for us to decide on the policy, for the present, of spreading guerrilla warfare far and wide and setting up temporary base areas in the plains. . . .[40]

Such seasonal base areas might be compared in wei-ch'i to seemingly dead groups which, as a result of changed strategic conditions, suddenly spring to life again (a frequent occurrence).[41] In this regard, it is amusing to contrast Mao's wei-ch'i complexity with Jomini's chesslike simplicity when the French theorist wrote: "The front of operations, being the space which separates the two armies and upon which

109

they may fight, is ordinarily parallel to the base of operations. It . . . ought to be perpendicular to the principal line
of operations. . . ." [42]

PROTRACTED WAR, PROTRACTED GAME

In 1938, Mao Tse-tung delivered a series of lectures at the
Yenan Staff College which were later published in book
form under the title *On Protracted War*. In this volume, the
Communist leader set forth, on the basis of the military and
political situation in 1938, a general plan for defense against
the Japanese invasion of China. Although his program was
never implemented except in Communist-controlled areas, it
has often been considered the theoretical basis of all Chinese Communist strategy. It, therefore, deserves detailed
comparison with wei-ch'i.

The defense of China against the Japanese should, in
Mao's view, consist of three successive phases. In the first
phase, the entire nation would be on the strategic defensive,
and the Japanese would acquire large, if unsubstantial,
spheres of influence extending inland from the coast; in the
second, a stalemate would ensue; while, by the third, the
Chinese player would be able to go over to the strategic
offensive. It is fruitful to compare these three stages to the
opening, the middle, and the end, respectively, of a two-
player handicap wei-ch'i game, the Chinese having the
handicap.[43]

When Mao developed his defense/counteroffense model
in 1938, the game had already begun. The Japanese invasion of China was like the opening of a conflict on a wei-ch'i
board already partially occupied by the stones of the handicap (the Chinese) player. The Chinese handicap was not,
however, strong enough, as Mao perceived, to prevent the
Japanese from gaining considerable territory: China, he

stressed, had failed to mobilize and to prepare itself for the war. As a result, the strategy to which the Nationalists inclined, that of defending China's coast in an attempt at positional containment of the invaders, had the disastrous results which ensue when (as frequently happens) a wei-ch'i novice feels himself motivated to try to dominate the *entire* board.[44] The purpose of Mao's theory of protracted war was to present an alternate plan of national defense.

The theory of protracted war proceeded from the valid assumption that Japanese strategy was to seize control of the heartland of China: in wei-ch'i terms, the center of the human and of the geographic—especially the geographic—boards, as often seems desirable to the wei-ch'i beginner. The Chinese player should then attempt to capitalize in a wei-ch'i fashion on the mistaken strategy of the opponent. Mao believed that the most efficient way to capitalize was to play around the edges of both the political and the military boards and to cede, at least temporarily, the apparently impressive center territories to the Japanese. In particular, the Chinese player should adopt the strategically sound, if unspectacular, policy of consolidating firm bases of support among the Chinese masses—the edge of the human board. Moreover, the Chinese should also emphasize development of countryside base areas behind Japanese lines, as was actually achieved by the Chinese Communists. Utilizing these near-to-the-edge-of-the-board bases, the Chinese player could begin, at least operationally, to encircle and kill—even capture (in the wei-ch'i sense)—certain insecure Japanese groups. (Examples of "captures" may be seen in the September 1937 battle at the P'inghsing pass on the Hopei-Shansi border, when the Communists under Lin Piao scored a decisive victory over a Japanese brigade; and in the battle of Taierhchuang, near Hsuchow in east China in the spring of 1938, when Nationalist forces commanded by the

Kwangsi generals Li Tsung-jen and Pai Ch'ung-hsi destroyed an advancing Japanese column.) [45] During the first phase, however, the optimal strategy, as envisaged by Mao, completely avoided decisive battles and was designed to effect an opening of the game as in wei-ch'i rather than as in chess, either Chinese or Western.

In the second stage of the war, Mao felt a relative stalemate would ensue: a stalemate in which the impressive territories gained by the Japanese in the first stage would have been considerably reduced by guerrilla warfare but in which the Chinese would not yet be sufficiently strong to annihilate large Japanese groups. Chinese strategy in this phase would be similar to that of the wei-ch'i player in the middle game: exploitation of the jigsaw pattern to isolate and disconnect enemy groups; extension of influence toward the center; and other preparation for encirclement and annihilation yet to be realized. The principal pattern of force prevalent in this phase would be that discontinuity of deployment characteristic of the half-developed wei-ch'i game, already analyzed in the last section.[46]

On initial consideration, the similarity between the end game of wei-ch'i on the one hand and the third and last phase of protracted war as projected by Mao on the other is less apparent than are comparable analogies in the two previous stages. Mao and later Chinese Communist analysts envisioned the end phase of the war as final encirclement *and* annihilation of the enemy groups. The encirclement motif is excellent wei-ch'i strategy. But when Mao speaks of annihilation, however, a paradox appears: in wei-ch'i games between most players of comparable skill, the end game is devoted to minor expansion and consolidation, not to major operations of annihilation; and, as pointed out in Chapter I, both sides generally terminate the game with substantial amounts of territory and of stones to their credit. One way to resolve this paradox is if we recognize that Mao Tse-tung considered himself and his high command to be wei-ch'i masters, and the Japanese to be amateurs. To quote only one remark—rendered more significant by its brevity—in *On Protracted War*: ". . . much of the enemy's strategic and campaign command is incompetent. . . ." [47] Fortified with this assessment, it is no wonder that Mao confidently proposed the final annihilation of the enemy.

A similar situation prevails in wei-ch'i. When a master confronts a novice, even a novice with initial superiority deriving from a large handicap—and, in a sense, Japanese stones in China were a type of handicap relative to the game of the Chinese counteroffensive—the probable result is the complete rout of the inferior player. Major battles of annihilation last throughout the end game, far more than, for example, in chess. When even a second-rate player of some experience confronts a novice playing his first game, it may be expected that the amateur will, thanks to the slight superiority which strategic and tactical experience have given him, have complete domination over the board at the end of the game. [48] Given the *assumed* strength-differential between Chinese and Japanese strategy in the third stage, as well as in the preceding two stages, the protracted-war model proposed by Mao Tse-tung is merely applied and generalized wei-ch'i.

As for the validity of this assumption, whether accurate in application to Japanese strategy in the Second World War or not, its correctness can scarcely be questioned in the context of the final, post-1945 struggle between the Chinese Communists and the Nationalists.

113

●

FIVE

CIVIL WAR, 1945-1949

The third and last phase of the Chinese Communist rise to power began about July 1946, after the failure of the mission of General George C. Marshall which sought to prevent all-out struggle between Communist and Nationalist factions.[1] The strategic pattern of this decisive civil struggle again presents definite analogies to wei-ch'i. On the national level—the level of grand strategy—the pattern of operations was similar to that of the late middle and end game of wei-ch'i, especially to those stages of the game between players of significantly differing skills. On certain sub-national boards, however, Communist operations between 1945 and 1949 passed, in effect, through the complete wei-ch'i cycle, beginning with the opening and terminating with the end game.

In contrast to the analytic hypotheses presented in pre-

ceding chapters identifying the structure of pre-1945 insurgent strategy in China, treatment of the 1945–49 civil
war will be oriented toward a lower level of strategic abstraction. There are two reasons for this shift. First, and
more important, historical study of specific military campaigns for the post-1945 development of Chinese Communism exceeds that done for the pre-1945 period. While the
data are inadequate, they nevertheless permit battle-
campaign analysis such as is still impossible for earlier
phases of insurgency. Second, after 1945, the character of
Chinese Communist insurgent warfare underwent considerable change. Before that year, the pattern of operational
strategy was that of co-ordination of a multitude of small
units and of direction of the tasks of thousands of politico-
military cadres operating under relatively primitive
communication-transportation conditions. After 1945, Chinese Communist operations, though by no means analogous to the mechanized, armored, airborne warfare of the
Second World War in the West, tended to group units in
larger masses, to undertake and carry through larger battles,
and to acquire more of the adjuncts of the modern army:
radio, artillery, even tanks. As prelude to wei-ch'i analysis of
the resulting operational strategy, we first turn to a brief historical résumé of the final civil war period.[2]

HISTORICAL BACKGROUND

In terms of zones of control, the Sino-Japanese war ended
with Communist domination of most of the countryside of
north China—Shensi, Shansi, Hopei, and Shantung—and of
considerable areas in the central part of the country—
Kiangsu, Anhwei, and Honan (see Map 1 for province loca-
tions). Desirous of regaining prestigious strongpoints lost
eight years before to the Japanese, the Nationalists, at the

end of the war, initiated with United States aid a major shift of the strategic center of gravity to north China and, secondarily, to central China and Manchuria.[3] The result was what a reasonably acute observer might have anticipated. By the end of 1945, the Nationalists occupied positions in the areas just mentioned which were comparable to those held by the Japanese before them: in other words, the Nationalists held the cities and lines of communication; the Communists, the countryside. However, in certain respects, the Nationalist position was worse than that of the Japanese had been: in particular, the Japanese surrender had given the Communists, following Russian withdrawal to the north, an opportunity to occupy much of Manchuria, including such large cities as Harbin (see Map 7 for pattern of operations).[4]

Military operations in 1946 derived directly from the situation sketched above. In late 1945, the Nationalists made the decision to commit their best forces to Manchuria in an attempt to wrest this strategic region from Communist control. By the end of 1946, the Nationalists had occupied Kirin, Changchun, and Mukden, three of the four most populous cities in northeast China. To the south, they had succeeded in clearing Hupeh and southern Honan and had attempted, without success, to annihilate Communist forces in eastern Kiangsu. In north China, the Nationalists held various large cities in Hopei and Shansi (including its capital Taiyuan), though sometimes not the communication lines between them; and they controlled the Tsingtao-Tsinan railway in Shantung but little else in that province.

Three principal campaigns characterized the year 1947 (for the situation in March, see Map 8). In the west, the Nationalists attacked the main Communist base at Yenan in Shensi province; in the east, they mounted an offensive in Shantung; and, in the northeast, they attempted to expand control of Manchuria. The Nationalists did succeed in capturing the Communist capital of Yenan; the city, however, had been previously evacuated by the Communists, with the result that no tangible military success was gained by the Nationalists. In east China, Nationalist operations in Shantung likewise failed to encircle and annihilate the Communists as had been optimistically hoped. In August 1947, the Communist commanders again seized the initiative. The principal Communist forces in Hopei thrust southward in a drive which carried Communist units almost to the Yangtze valley. At the same time, the main Communist army evacuated Shantung to fill the vacuum in Hopei created by this southward move. Meanwhile, however, Communist guerrilla forces in Shantung continued attrition of Nationalist strength and morale. To the north in Manchuria, the Communists also scored major successes and threatened Nationalist communications in Jehol and Liaoning. In north China, the situation remained relatively static.

The year of decision was 1948. In the Manchurian theater, a Communist offensive in January finally succeeded in achieving the principal Communist objective in that region: isolation of the major Nationalist-controlled cities of Mukden, Changchun, and Kirin. After a siege of nine months, these last Nationalist positions in the northeast fell; and, with them, collapsed Nationalist hopes of strategic victory on the mainland. In north China, meanwhile, the Communists launched a strategic offensive which recaptured Yenan and even threatened Szechwan in the southwest. In Shansi province, Taiyuan, the last major Nationalist stronghold, was encircled in the autumn and fell in April 1949. In Shantung, the the Communists gained a major victory when Tsinan, capital and key Nationalist stronghold, fell. Thus, by late 1948, the Communists had control over most of north China—except the Peiping-Tientsin-Kalgan complex, which

Source: Adapted from *The Communist Conquest of China* by Lionel Max Chassin (Cambridge, Mass.: Harvard University Press). Copyright © 1965 by the President and Fellows of Harvard College. Reprinted by permission of the publishers.

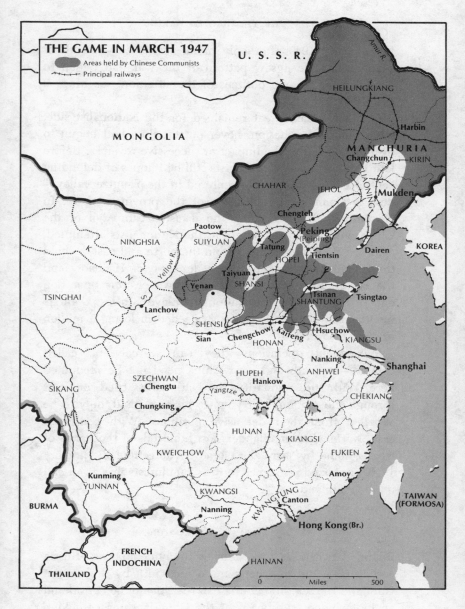

THE GAME IN MARCH 1947

Areas held by Chinese Communists

Principal railways

U. S. S. R.

Amur R.

MONGOLIA

HEILUNGKIANG

Harbin

MANCHURIA

Changchun — KIRIN

CHAHAR — JEHOL — LIAONING — **Mukden**

Chengteh

Paotow — Peking (Peiping)

NINGHSIA — SUIYUAN — Tatung — HOPEI — Tientsin — Dairen — KOREA

Yellow R.

Taiyuan — SHANSI

TSINGHAI — Yenan — Tsinan — SHANTUNG — Tsingtao

Lanchow

SHENSI

KANSU

Sian — Chengchow — Kaifeng — Hsuchow — KIANGSU

HONAN

Nanking — Shanghai

SZECHWAN — HUPEH — ANHWEI

Chengtu — Hankow

SIKANG — Yangtze — CHEKIANG

Chungking

HUNAN — KIANGSI — FUKIEN

KWEICHOW

Kunming — Amoy

YUNNAN

BURMA — KWANGSI — KWANGTUNG — Canton — TAIWAN (FORMOSA)

Nanning

Hong Kong (Br.)

FRENCH INDOCHINA

THAILAND — HAINAN

0 — Miles — 500

Map 8

Source: Adapted from *The Communist Conquest of China* by Lionel Max Chassin (Cambridge, Mass.: Harvard University Press). Copyright © 1965 by the President and Fellows of Harvard College. Reprinted by permission of the publishers.

fell in early 1949 after only minor resistance—and all of Manchuria. The jigsaw pattern of the war had begun to clarify. (For general outlines of the situation, see Maps 9 and 10.)

One last great defeat remained for the Nationalist side, whose internal cohesion, never outstanding, had begun to disintegrate under the impact of successive reverses. Before late 1948, Nationalist strategists still had hopes of defending central China—the region centered in the Yangtze valley—despite Communist infiltration of the provinces there. In November 1948, therefore, the decisive campaign of the Chinese civil war was fought as the Nationalists attempted, against Communist attacks from the north and east, to hold the region between the railway junction of Hsuchow and the ocean. Like its predecessors, however, this operation ended in failure for the Nationalist player: in less than six months, the Nationalist army succeeded in losing a million or more troops.

Subsequent operations—they can scarcely be called combat—in south and west China need not be recounted here. With sure regularity, the Nationalists tried, or went through the motions of trying, to make a stand, only to be expelled from their defensive positions. With consistent ease, Nationalist commanders lost hundreds of thousands of troops, some by surrender, some by defection. By January 1950, organized resistance to the Communists was at an end on the mainland.

THE GAME IN MANCHURIA

Bounded as it is on three sides by foreign countries—Russia and Korea—and in great part to the south by the eastern Gobi and the sea, Manchuria can realistically be considered an independent sub-board of the China theater (see Map

THE GAME IN MAY 1948

Areas held by Communists
Comunist attacks
Nationalist attacks
Communist guerrillas
(Note the scattered stones in south China)

U. S. S. R.

MONGOLIA

HEILUNGKIANG

MANCHURIA

KIRIN
Changchun

CHAHAR
JEHOL
Mukden

NINGHSIA
SUIYUAN
Paotow
Tatung
Peking
(Peiping)
Dairen
KOREA

Taiyuan
HOPEI
Tientsin

TSINGHAI
Yenan
SHANSI
Tsinan
SHANTUNG
Tsingtao

Lanchow
Sian
Loyang
Kaifeng
Hsuchow
KIANGSU

SHENSI
HONAN
Nanking
Shanghai

SIKANG
SZECHWAN
Chengtu
HUPEH
Hankow
ANHWEI
CHEKIANG

Chungking
Yangtze

HUNAN
KIANGSI
FUKIEN

KWEICHOW
Amoy

Kunming
YUNNAN
West R.
KWANGTUNG
Canton
TAIWAN
(FORMOSA)

BURMA
Nanning
Hong Kong (Br.)

FRENCH
INDOCHINA
HAINAN
0   Miles   500

SIAM
(THAILAND)

MAP 9

Source: Adapted from *The Communist Conquest of China* by Lionel Max Chassin (Cambridge, Mass.: Harvard University Press). Copyright © 1965 by the President and Fellows of Harvard College. Reprinted by permission of the publishers.

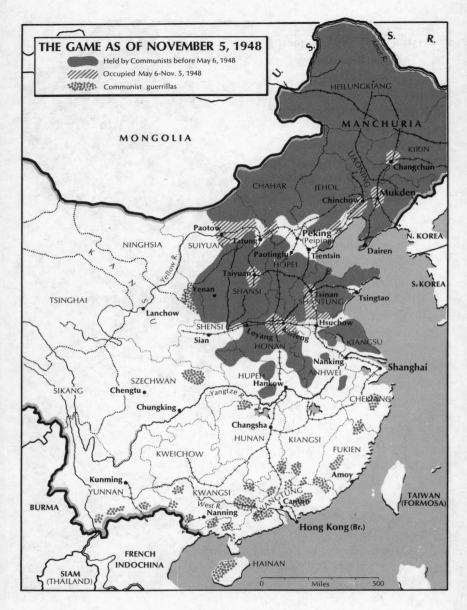

THE GAME AS OF NOVEMBER 5, 1948

Held by Communists before May 6, 1948
Occupied May 6-Nov. 5, 1948
Communist guerrillas

MAP 10

Source: Adapted from *The Communist Conquest of China* by Lionel Max Chassin (Cambridge, Mass.: Harvard University Press). Copyright © 1965 by the President and Fellows of Harvard College. Reprinted by permission of the publishers.

11). In consequence, it is natural to view operations and strategy on that board as a generally independent subsystem of war and politics on the national level.[5]

In the first half of the year 1945, two sides—Communist and Japanese—sought to play stones and to secure territory and influence on the Manchurian boards. Communist efforts in this theater during the pre-1945 period were not, however, as successful as in north and central China. ". . . there is not yet the wide base of popular support for the [Communist] movement that there was . . . in North China," stated the Communist general Lin Piao as late as 1946.[6] In early 1945, therefore, the game in Manchuria might be termed relatively latent.

In August of that year, the Soviet Union declared war on Japan and invaded Manchuria. When Soviet occupation forces withdrew some nine months later, in May 1946, the Chinese Communists who, with some Soviet aid, had been assiduously playing stones on the northeastern board, were left confronting a new player, the Nationalists. This last player was intent on seizing control of the rich Manchurian region, though its industrial plants had been stripped by the Russians. By early 1946, the Communists already possessed a large but unconsolidated territory, or rather sphere of influence, both political and military, in north and west Manchuria; whereas Nationalist strength gravitated around the south and central areas of the board, including the cities of Mukden and Changchun. Nationalist military forces in Manchuria at this stage of the game numbered about 150,000; the Communists, by their own claim, over twice that figure.

This strategic situation, if we interpret nearness to the edge of the board literally (as may, in fact, be plausibly done, since the urban-industrial pivot of Manchuria lies on its central plain), might be likened to the opening of a wei-

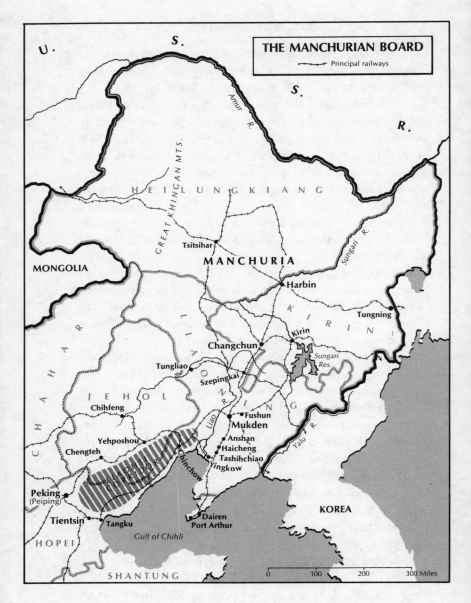

MAP 11

ch'i game in which one player has the bulk of his stones placed at the top of the board and along the adjoining sides, while the opponent's men are displaced along the lower edge. An example of an actual game with such a strategic pattern may be found in the sixth world-championship match played in 1951. Diagram 18 shows the respective positions of White and Black after nine moves. If the board is rotated counter-clockwise at a 90 degree angle, the situation of Black might be compared to that of the Communists in Manchuria in early 1946; that of White, to the Nationalist position.[7] It is interesting to note the Japanese master Takagawa's comment on this position: ". . . it cannot be denied that White is late and has allowed his opponent to get a start over him." [8]

As stated above, the strategic objective of the Nationalists in Manchuria—the motivation for deployment far from a secure base—was control of the main cities, industrial areas, and communications of that highly developed ex-Japanese region and, very secondarily, control of the countryside, the topographic edge of the board. The Communist objective was to gain control of the whole board by encirclement and annihilation of the Nationalist armies. The solution of the problem provides an interesting, and far from trivial, parallel with wei-ch'i strategy.

Before the Communist player could achieve his ultimate strategic goal, however, he had to attain its defensive equivalent: the arrest of the Nationalist northward drive against Communist stones and bases on the northern bank of the Sungari river (see Map 11).

By early June of 1946, the Nationalist advance based at Changchun held a bridgehead on the north bank of the Sungari, and Nationalist commanders were preparing for a drive on Harbin. Like good wei-ch'i players, the Communist generals combated direction with indirection. Instead of

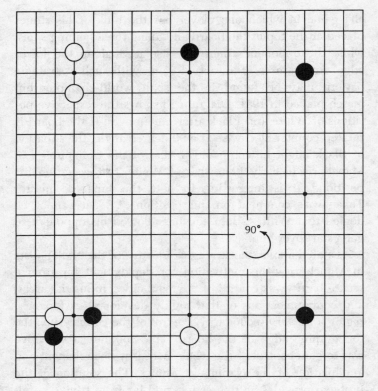

DIAGRAM 18

Source: Adapted from *The Vital Points of Go* by Kaku Takagawa (Tokyo: Japanese Go Association). Reprinted by permission.

undertaking a positional defense in northern Manchuria and concentrating all available stones at the apparently decisive point, the Communists threatened the Liaohsi corridor in an offensive aimed at severing the communications of Nationalist groups in Manchuria from those in Hopei. The Communists captured Anshan, Haicheng, and Tashihchiao to the east and threatened Yingkow, the port through which Nationalist armies to the north were supplied. On the other

126

side of the corridor, the insurgents cut the Chihfeng-Yehposhou railroad line. Both offensives were minor and fairly direct in approach. The threat to their communications, however, caused the Nationalist commanders to rush reinforcements from the north to recapture the lost towns. Further Nationalist advances in the north were precluded by a truce effective on June 7, 1946.

In July, after the end of this ill-fated cease-fire, the Nationalists, realizing the fragility of their line of communication via the Liaohsi corridor, began to play stones in Jehol province and occupied Kalgan. "Beware," says the wei-ch'i proverb, "of going back to patch up your plays." [9]

In February 1947, the Communists reacted to Nationalist preoccupation in the south by making their first direct major offensive against Nationalist units preparing for operations designed for the capture of Harbin. Attacking at Tungliao, the Communists outflanked Nationalist displacements and moved 270,000 men into central Manchuria to encircle a Nationalist army retreating to Ssupingkai. This outflanking and encirclement process was similar to the wei-ch'i situation in which a player strikes at his opponent's weak flank in order to minimize the effectiveness of a frontal drive: "to reduce [a potential] territory, strike at the shoulder." [10]

In the same phase of operations, Communist attacks on the Liaohsi corridor intensified. A Communist offensive, using the Jehol-Liaohsi border area as a base, recaptured Jehol. In early June, another force attacked on the southern Liao river, which divides the province of Liaoning in half. Both offensives were aimed at gradually tightening Communist encirclement of Nationalist areas in north-central Manchuria and, as such, were wei-ch'i disconnecting operations. It is significant that, taken in conjunction, the two offensives threatened both sides of the Liaohsi corridor almost simultaneously: in wei-ch'i, a complex disconnecting

127

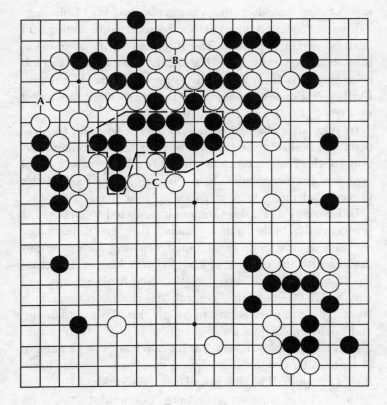

DIAGRAM 19

Source: From *Go and Go-moku* by Edward Lasker (New York: Dover Publications, Inc., 1960). Reprinted by permission of the publisher.

operation usually requires attack on both sides of the enemy forces.[11]

Although Nationalist counterattacks soon impelled minor and temporary Communist withdrawals on all fronts, such withdrawals did not eliminate Communist strategic gains. Communist lines had moved 150 miles south during the spring of 1947, and Changchun, Kirin, and Mukden were mutually isolated, with connecting railway lines destroyed.

128

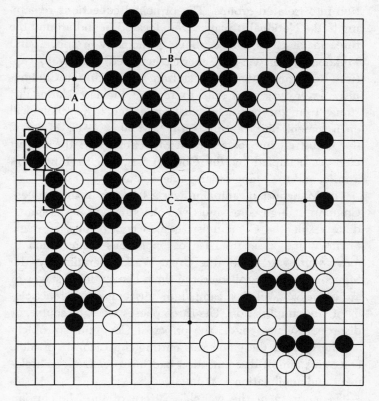

DIAGRAM 20

Source: From *Go and Go-moku* by Edward Lasker (New York: Dover Publications, Inc., 1960). Reprinted by permission of the publisher.

The Communists then began the final stage of the Manchurian game. In January 1948, they attacked the Liaohsi corridor once more and formed a connected group across it, roughly perpendicular to the Peking-Mukden railway which was the main axis of Nationalist communications. In wei-ch'i terms, the conflict pattern began to simplify with the crystallization of the Communist position into a connected structure and with the disintegration of the Nationalist position into isolated groups. The principal collections remaining to the Nationalist player were located in and around the three major cities named above, principally in and around Mukden. As in wei-ch'i, encirclement led directly to capture. Repulsing counterattacks from the south, the Communist player was soon able to remove the last Nationalist stones from the board by what amounted to psychological encirclement and capture.[12] In November 1948, Mukden, the industrial hub of southern Manchuria and the largest city yet occupied by the Communists, fell to Lin Piao's armies, and the Manchurian game was over.

The Manchurian campaign was a triumph of the Chinese Communist high command's wei-ch'i strategy. As its immediate result, the Communists gained control of a strategic territory and a secure base of operations from which to move southward inside the Great Wall. Operationally, the Manchurian game followed the three conventional stages of an offensive wei-ch'i campaign: disconnection, encirclement, and annihilation. The three phases were, of course, of disproportionate length: the principal Communist problem for the bulk of the game was cutting the Liaohsi corridor. Once this aim of disconnection had been realized, encirclement and annihilation soon followed.[13]

The entirety of the wei-ch'i pattern of the Manchurian game may be clarified by comparing it with that of the operations depicted in Diagrams 19–21. In Diagram 19, Black, the Nationalist player, has a large collection in the center of the board (indicated by an encircling line) which, however, has structurally weak communications with Black bases to the "south," that is, those near the bottom of the board. These communications are made more insecure by the presence of powerful White collections to the north and west (A and B in the diagram) and by the guerrilla group C. Diagram 20 shows the situation some 25 moves of

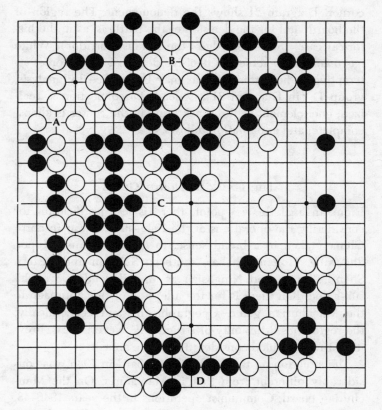

DIAGRAM 21

game-time later. By continuous exertion of pressure, White, the Communist player, has managed to initiate heavy attacks on Black's southwest communication lines and to kill the circled groups. Note that the guerrillas around C have played an important role by preventing contact between the center Black forces and those in the lower right (southeast) corner. Diagram 21 shows the denouement. The region of the board vital for the decision of the battle is, as in the historical case, the lower edge (the Liaohsi corridor). White has managed to achieve a decisive defeat of Black forces attempting to hold this area; as may be verified by analysis, group D (in Diagram 21) is dead. Disconnection is realized; encirclement of the Black army in the center is almost complete; and annihilation follows.[14]

THE GAME IN NORTH CHINA

From an analytic viewpoint, there is less justification for considering the operations of the 1945–49 civil war in north China (taken in a broad sense, to include Shansi, Hopei, Shantung, Honan, Chahar, southern Suiyuan and eastern Shensi, Kansu, and Ninghsia) as an independent wei-ch'i sub-game than there is for the adoption of this approach to the Manchurian game. Geographically and economically, the region has little unity of structure.[15] Nevertheless, brevity warrants unified consideration of the area.

The situation on the north China board in 1946 was considerably different from that in Manchuria. On the Manchurian board, Communist operations in the years 1946–48, as we have seen, went through what was, in effect, the entire wei-ch'i cycle from opening to end game; on the north China board, the Communist player possessed numerous bases and stones dating back as far as 1937 and developed throughout the entire Sino-Japanese war. On the north China board, therefore, strategic time was, in a sense, more advanced than farther to the north (an unevenness frequently characteristic of the wei-ch'i game and another manifestation of its jigsaw pattern).

On the political level, many rural areas of north China

had been under Communist control for years, and the populace was psychologically encircled in the sense described in the preceding chapter.[16] On the geographic board, by far the majority of the approximately one million Communist regular and irregular soldiers on the China board at the end of the Second World War were located in the provinces of north China enumerated above and, at least during the crucial months following the Japanese surrender, far outnumbered Nationalist forces in those regions. In wei-ch'i terms, although the Nationalists, aided by American transport facilities, soon occupied most major cities and rail lines, the Communists, from the beginning of the period under consideration, possessed secure edge-of-the-board bases and were able to use them in the encirclement of the center.

In the light of this situation, we may divide north and northwest China operations of the 1946–48 period into two categories: first, those characterized by Communist attrition of positional Nationalist defenses; second, those based upon Communist-Nationalist confrontation in the field. This dichotomy distinguishes, in effect, between the statics and the dynamics of Chinese Communist revolutionary warfare.

Typical of the first type of operation were hostilities in Shansi and in Hopei. In these areas, the civil war revolved around Communist attack and Nationalist defense of two types of center-of-the-board strongpoints: cities and railroads. The reason for gradual Communist success in attrition of Nationalist forces occupying these areas may be explained by wei-ch'i theory, as might the relatively slow tempo with which the Communists made progress. A Nationalist-occupied city was like a single intersection occupied by a single stone (the garrison force), except when outposts were occasionally put out, in which case city and outposts might be compared to a two-stone group or other small wei-ch'i formation. Railroad defenses were lines of stones, linear groups, or rather linear collections, since in practice a railroad was defended only by a series of discrete strongpoints.

Like their wei-ch'i analogues, these center-of-the-board Nationalist groups, even though they did disseminate influence and often posed potential threats to Communist communications, did not encircle territory. In wei-ch'i theory, it is axiomatic that, during the middle game, the isolated point-force (stone, or small group) or linear-line force (chain of stones) located five or more intersections from the edge of the board cannot *of itself* acquire territory.[17] Co-ordination of force in depth is necessary for territorial control; and, in the north China position, Nationalist-controlled points or lines were often fifty or one hundred miles apart, with strong Communist forces—in depth and supported by solid political territory—intervening. Nor was the Nationalist position improved by the strategy which Nationalist commanders customarily employed, a strategy characterized by inertia or timidity which failed to provide for aggressive patrols or for extensions (to use the wei-ch'i idiom) into the countryside, with a city or a railroad used as base.[18] Nationalist performance tended, therefore, to accentuate the zero or uni-dimensionality of the strategic deployment which the Nationalist commanders favored.

The wei-ch'i consequences of the Nationalist position are not difficult to assess. Safety in wei-ch'i implies control of at least a modicum of territory—a quantity in excess of what the Nationalists generally held. As a result, the Communist player was in position to capture—that is, overrun— Nationalist positions, one by one, as military exigencies dictated. At the same time, however, as in wei-ch'i, actual capture of Nationalist groups—such as Taiyuan, long since dead—would have been a dissipation of Communist energies. In many cases, therefore, the Communists adopted the strategy of isolating the enemy and of waiting for inevitable surrender: in the paradoxical vocabulary of wei-ch'i, a policy of "kill rather than capture." An excellent illustration of this technique was the Communist take-over of the Peiping-Tientsin area in early 1949: after a long period of semidormancy, dead Nationalist stones were pacifically "removed" from the military board by the surrender of their commander Fu Tso-yi.

Turning from statics to dynamics, an entirely different type of situation arises. When the Nationalists took to the field, either on offense or defense, the Communist adopted an aggressive strategy of encirclement and annihilation, frequently tempered by extensive use of a wei-ch'i indirect approach. Two interesting campaigns of this nature took place in north China in 1947 and 1948: one was fought in the northwest around Yenan; the other, in east China and Shantung.

The Nationalist offensive against the wartime Communist capital of Yenan had an auspicious start, for little Communist resistance was offered against the initial Nationalist drive. The good wei-ch'i player, as already stressed, never feels responsible for controlling a region whose defense he feels to be valueless. Rather than taking up a defensive position in the Yenan area, the Communists adopted their time-honored wei-ch'i expedient of playing their stones considerably in advance of the oncoming Nationalists and of awaiting an opportunity for counterattack. Again, wei-ch'i strategy proved adequate to the situation. Once Yenan had been occupied by the Nationalists, their advance beyond the city was checked by the threat of Communist groups in the west, in what by then amounted to the Nationalist rear; and, by early 1948, the Communists succeeded in forcing their opponent to evacuate Yenan and in gaining control of most of Shensi. In a sense, the operation was militarily insignificant in relation to the entire military situation in China and in comparison to more dramatic battles in which hundreds of thousands of Nationalist stones were captured. As an example of wei-ch'i pattern, however, aspects of the development of the operation furnish a relevant lesson.

In Maoist strategic conflicts, as in wei-ch'i, a frontal, columnar assault such as that of the Nationalists against Yenan is dangerous only to a defender on exterior lines. When the defender is on interior lines—as were the Communists in Shensi with a mobilized populace and other bases nearby, or as is a wei-ch'i player in a corner base—a unidimensional direct incision is generally as useless to the attacker as it is harmless to the attacked. Refer, for instance, to Diagram 22 A. In the situation portrayed, Black uses three plays to occupy a hollow in the White defense. This operation *in itself* is not injurious to Black's self-interest. When, however, the three completely unchallenged moves that White has been able to make somewhere on the board are considered, Black's offensive appears decidedly disadvantageous (these moves are not shown in the diagram because the full position is not given).[19] This wei-ch'i situation symbolizes the frustrations which plagued the Nationalists in the course of the Yenan campaign.[20]

While the Nationalists were employing elite troops to hold Yenan, a far more decisive campaign was being waged on the other side of the board whose unfavorable outcome for the Nationalists was influenced by their concentration of valuable stones to the west. The basic maneuvers were as follows (refer to Map 12 for place names and rail lines): The Nationalist objective was to gain control of Tsinan, Tsingtao, and Hsuchow, with connecting rail lines, so as to form what would amount to a net of stones to trap the Communist force in Shantung operating south and east of railways to the Yellow Sea. In fact, the Nationalists

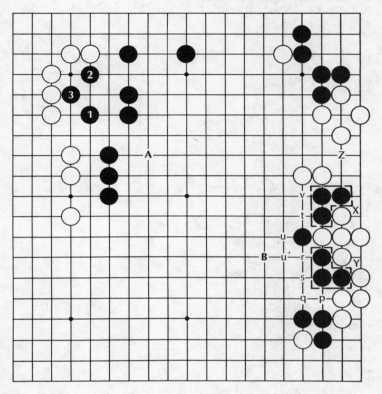

DIAGRAM 22

achieved most of their objective: by February-March 1947, they had linked up Tsinan and Tsingtao and had pushed far north of Hsuchow on the railway connecting that city with Tsinan. In early March, however, just as Nationalist success seemed assured, the Communist high command made a key strategic decision, the most critical on the Communist side of the campaign. This command decision involved two orders. First, Communist forces under Liu Po-ch'eng, based in Hopei, moved to threaten Hsuchow and the Nationalist rear

137

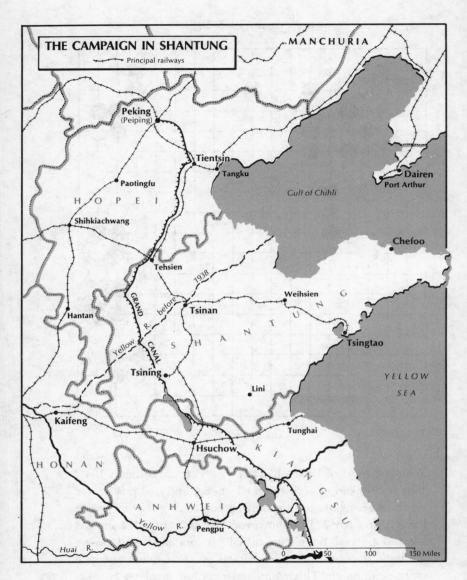

THE CAMPAIGN IN SHANTUNG

⊢⊣ Principal railways

MANCHURIA

Peking
(Peiping)

Tientsin

Tangku

Gulf of Chihli

Dairen
Port Arthur

H O P E I

Paotingfu

Chefoo

Shihkiachwang

Tehsien

Weihsien

Tsinan

Hantan

Tsingtao

S H A N T U N G

Tsining

Lini

YELLOW
SEA

Kaifeng

Tunghai

Hsuchow

H O N A N

K I A N G S U

A N H W E I

Yellow R.

Pengpu

Huai R.

0   50   100   150 Miles

Map 12

from the southwest. Almost simultaneously, following the second directive, the principal Communist forces in Shantung, under Ch'en Yi, shifted their center of gravity northward into northern Shantung and southern Hopei. Faced with a dual threat from the north and from the southwest, the Nationalist drive slowed to a standstill. The initiative lost, the Nationalist forces in Shantung and adjoining regions were reduced to a defensive role which culminated in eventual collapse.[21]

In a sense, the pattern just sketched is not uniquely identifiable with wei-ch'i strategy: by almost any reasonable strategic decision calculus, Communist strategic planning and implementation in the Shantung campaign achieved a high order of excellence. On the other hand, because the situation which that strategy was designed to exploit contained the basic wei-ch'i elements of discontinuity and jigsaw pattern, it seems relevant to parallel Communist strategy with a concrete example of good wei-ch'i illustrated in Diagram 22 B—if only to demonstrate that, in paraconventional as in purely guerrilla warfare, Chinese Communist strategy has underlying wei-ch'i dynamics.

In the diagram, taken from an amateur wei-ch'i game, Black corresponds to the Nationalists; White, to the "Red bandits." In the position shown, the Black stone immediately to the right of u has apparently almost realized union of Black groups X and Y (Tsinan-Tsingtao and Hsuchow-Lini, respectively) in co-ordinated encirclement of the White group sandwiched along the edge of the board (the Communist army of Ch'en Yi with its rear to the Yellow Sea). The White group at Z represents the Communist army in northern Shantung and southern Hopei, with the empty region to the left representing eastern Honan and northern Kiangsu-Anhwei (review Map 12). The enemy seemingly cornered, Black is now confronted with the following gambit. White plays at p. Black contains break-out at q. White plays at r, "southwest of Hsuchow." Black is forced to retreat with s. Continuing pressure, White strikes at t. Black's stone, now encircled on three sides, is forced to respond either by extension at u or at u'. White moves his weight north at v. This last development is the climax. As can be shown by analysis of the entire position, the Tsinan group is dead, and Black's position disintegrates. As in the historical case, the key move in this sequence was r, initial precursor of the cumulative, indirect, but highly effective pressure so characteristic of the wei-ch'i method.

THE GAME IN CENTRAL CHINA: THE HUAI-HAI BATTLE

Growing directly out of the results of the Shantung campaign of early 1948 was what may be termed the critical encounter of the Chinese civil war: the Huai-Hai battle.[22] By mid-1948, Nationalist defeat to the north—in Manchuria and north China—either was already history or was imminent. There remained the board of east-central China between the Communist-controlled north and the surviving pivot of Nationalist power south of the Yangtze.

In Manchuria and north China, Nationalist operations and their Communist counterparts are difficult to reduce to the simple linear pattern characteristic of Western warfare since ancient times: this is the phenomenon of jigsaw pattern already much discussed. By late 1948, however, the dialectical structure of the war was becoming simplified; the remaining loci of living (in the wei-ch'i sense) Nationalist power were relatively linear along the central China axis just mentioned. (See Map 10 for details; of course, nonlinearity is still strongly marked, but disregarding Communist guerrillas on the east China coast and scattered regions of Communist control in the south, it would still be possible to trace a rough front line for the Nationalists, as would not have been possible in early May: see Map 9.) In central China, therefore, Nationalist strategy may be interpreted as revolving around the attempted formation of a line, a front in the First World War sense, to contain the Communist armies to the north; in analogic wei-ch'i terms, a linear group.

Although certain Nationalist strategists felt that the line should be formed along the Huai river (see Map 13 for outlines of the campaign, somewhat over-linearized and simplified), Chiang Kai-shek overruled them and decreed that the decisive battle should be fought one hundred miles to the north of the river, around Hsuchow and along the Lunghai and Tientsin-Pukow railroads.[23] From the wei-ch'i point of view, the Nationalist strategists were probably correct: not only did the Huai river constitute a natural line of stones, but also the decision to withdraw to that river would have been similar to a decision in wei-ch'i, frequently lauded in earlier chapters, to form a defensive line several intersections distant from the opponent's main forces. Hsuchow and the line parallel to it and perpendicular to the seacoast constituted intersections dangerously close to large Communist groups (see Map 12). In the Huai-Hai battle, therefore, one of the principal factors in the Nationalist defeat was that the Nationalists played their stones too close to those of their Communist opponent, with the result that the Nationalist positions were overrun before a firm, consolidated front could be established. Hsuchow was an exposed salient. Powerful Communist collections to the northeast, in conjunction with Liu Po-ch'eng's 450,000 troops on the west, encircled Hsuchow on two sides.

On November 6, 1948, the Huai-Hai battle was joined with a Communist attack to the west of the pivotal city (see Map 13). The next day, November 7, the Communists

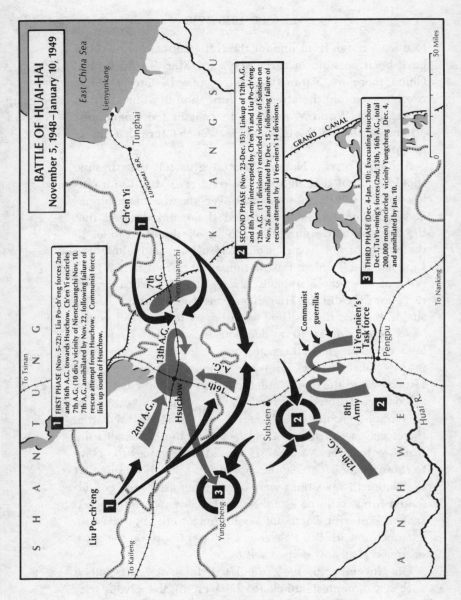

BATTLE OF HUAI-HAI
November 5, 1948–January 10, 1949

1 FIRST PHASE (Nov. 5-22): Liu Po-ch'eng forces 2nd and 16th A.G. towards Hsuchow. Ch'en Yi encircles 7th A.G. (10 div.) vicinity of Nienchuangchi Nov. 10. 7th A.G. annihilated by Nov. 22, following failure of rescue attempt from Hsuchow. Communist forces link up south of Hsuchow.

2 SECOND PHASE (Nov. 23-Dec. 15): Linkup of 12th A.G. and 8th Army intercepted by Ch'en Yi and Liu Po-ch'eng. 12th A.G. (11 divisions) encircled vicinity of Suhsien on Nov. 26 and annihilated by Dec. 15, following failure of rescue attempt by Li Yen-nien's 14 divisions.

3 THIRD PHASE (Dec. 4-Jan. 10): Evacuating Huchow Dec.1, Tu Yu-ming's forces(2nd, 13th, 16th A.G., total 200,000 men) encircled vicinity Yungcheng Dec. 4, and annihilated by Jan. 10.

MAP 13

Source: Adapted from *The Communist Conquest of China* by Lionel Max Chassin (Cambridge, Mass.: Harvard University Press). Copyright © 1965 by the President and Fellows of Harvard College. Reprinted by permission of the publishers.

broke through, pushing a Nationalist army group back to the west of Hsuchow. Three days later, the Communist player struck again, this time at the Nationalist flank to the east, and wedged several columns between the forces occupying Hsuchow and the Nationalist Seventh Army Group. In wei-ch'i fashion, the Communists had succeeded in placing several stones between key Nationalist strongpoints, rendering them incapable of giving each other direct assistance for the remainder of the campaign.

The Nationalist Seventh Army Group, which had thus been cut off from Hsuchow proper, tried to restore its position by pulling away from the East China Sea and shifting its center of gravity toward the city. Excellent intelligence, however, soon informed the Communist command of this movement, and the Seventh Army Group was rapidly encircled by forces inserted between its nucleus and the sea. The two army groups which Chiang ordered to relieve the Seventh were delayed.[24] Ten days after the Communist encirclement began, relieving units were still twelve miles from the outlying positions of the beleaguered force. To make matters more critical, the Communists, in conjunction with guerrillas already widespread in the entire theater, soon severed Nationalist communications to the south of Hsuchow. The Sixth Army Group (not shown on Map 13) to the west retreated like a wei-ch'i group attempting to save itself. The Second, Seventh, Thirteenth, and Sixteenth army groups, on the other hand, were trapped in and around Hsuchow in what has been likened to a "T" with the right crossbar (the Seventh Army Group) severed.[25] Hsuchow was encircled.

On November 22, the Communists succeeded in capturing the right half of the "T": the Seventh Army Group, isolated without new supplies for twelve days. Additional Nationalist forces to the south, ordered to relieve the Hsuchow

143

situation, either were themselves encircled by the Communists or were forced to retreat (see Map 13). By November 25, the Communists had managed to play new stones—in military strength, about a quarter of a million men—across Hsuchow's rail communications to the south. Encirclement led to annihilation: by early January of 1949, after a month and a half of uneven and strategically meaningless resistance, all Nationalist units in and around Hsuchow, including the elite Armored Corps which contained almost all Nationalist mechanized equipment, had been captured.[26]

There, baldly summarized, are the principal events, superimposed upon a wei-ch'i grid, of one of the most decisive military campaigns of modern history. It remains to draw theoretical conclusions.

Abstractly formulated, the lesson is as follows: no attempted linear deployment to contain an enemy operating on interior lines can be realized by a force operating on exterior lines, without strong proximate bases of support. (The actual logistical bases used by the Nationalists during the Huai-Hai campaign were in the Yangtze valley, some two hundred miles to the south; their politically secure territories were located virtually at infinity.) Any attempt to deploy in this manner and for this objective will result in the immediate (the Huai-Hai battle, in its active phase, lasted less than a month) encirclement and annihilation of a large part of the defending groups. Thus formulated, these strategic principles of wei-ch'i theory seem tautologous. In practice, however, the concept of containing the enemy, of stopping him without giving an unnecessary foot of ground, of never turning one's back on the foe, is basic to many systems of strategic ethics, both Western and non-Western: military history abounds with examples of the effect on combat operations of these notions. Any reasonable commander will, of course, recognize the occasional necessity of tactical retreat; but few indeed are the commanders who adopt the wei-ch'i principle of operational fluidity as completely as did the Chinese Communist top command. The Huai-Hai battle furnishes an example of the head-on collision, not merely of two armies, but of two systems of strategic thought. Its implications extend beyond the Communist victory on the Chinese mainland into the higher realms of military philosophy.

The Huai-Hai battle was the decisive campaign of the Communists' rise to national power. Despite the relative unimportance of the operations in south China which followed in the early months of 1949 and extended through early 1950, it is relevant to note at least one wei-ch'i analogue to a specific strategic motif extensively used in this period by the Communists. This technique is well described in a comprehensive treatment of counterinsurgency warfare:

> The basic operational principle to eliminate guerrillas who are few in number and isolated from the population is to force them to move, to become "roving bandits," and to catch them as they attempt to cross successive nets of counterinsurgent forces. Such were, in essence, the tactics followed with great success by the Chinese Communists themselves in south China in 1950–52, when they liquidated the Nationalist remnants.[27]

This technique of successive nets is similar to that used to defend a wei-ch'i territory in the end game and to prevent dead stones in the territory from forming safe groups: the partition of a given territory into sub-territories by chains of stones which force enemy groups contained within the net to flee until they become so encircled as to have no hope of future life.[28]

THE PRINCIPLES OF REVOLUTIONARY STRATEGY, 1945–49

In the opinion of some analysts of Chinese Communism, the strategy employed by the Chinese Communists before 1945 differed from that used after 1945 just as unconventional differs from conventional warfare, or as guerrilla operations differ from Napoleonic mobile strategy.[29] Before 1945, Chinese Communist strategy was (with a few exceptions) either defensive, or territory-making in the wei-ch'i sense; after that date, it was primarily oriented to offensive operations. Before 1945, it was a strategy which depended upon small and medium-sized units; after 1945, it progressively came to plan in terms of armies and army groups. Despite changes of Communist strategy in direction and degree, however, the wei-ch'i model remains as applicable after the Japanese surrender in 1945 as before. In accordance with wei-ch'i's protracted character—and in contrast to many Western games of strategy such as chess—the early phases of the game are invariably devoted to preparation for future offensives and to acquisition of fundamental territory rather than to actual killing and capturing. In the Chinese Communist insurgency, the Kiangsi period and the Sino-Japanese war represented the period of preparation. Subsequently in the course of the wei-ch'i game, especially when one player is markedly inferior in competence to his opponent, a transformation in the character of operations is brought about by the increasing readiness of the superior player to employ his better positioned and developed forces in decisive offensive action.[30]

In the historical case, the 1945–49 civil war was a corresponding phase of decision. The strategy employed in the insurgency, like the strategy used in the game, was a dynamic variable relative to time whose development was subject to constant guiding concepts.

The similarity in pattern between the decisive stage of a wei-ch'i game and the development of Chinese Communist power after 1945 lies in the structure of the offensive employed in both forms of conflict. In the Chinese Communist insurgency, the first stage of an offensive was disconnection or isolation. Communist forces struck at railways, roads, and other lines of Nationalist communication, harassing the enemy flanks and rear. Similarly, in wei-ch'i, the point of departure for all serious offensives must be the disconnection of the attacked group from all secure bases: by the structure of the capture, if the defender can link up with a safe territory, the offensive is automatically unsuccessful.

The second stage in an offensive was encirclement, a term too basic to wei-ch'i to require elaboration. As in wei-ch'i, encirclement tended to grow logically and gradually out of the stage of isolation, with the crude envelopment of enemy units growing into tight encirclement. Both in revolutionary warfare as practiced by Chinese Communist commanders and in the game of wei-ch'i, encirclement often originates and develops in a subtle manner, frequently emanating from an apparently passive territory (base area) or from the co-ordinated outcome of several scattered engagements. "Why are they attacking there?" Nationalist officers would often ask each other. ". . . there is no pattern, no sense to the Red web of strategy." [31] Yet a series of apparently meaningless Communist forays and attacks often culminated in encirclement of the very units which these puzzled Nationalists commanded. In both revolutionary war and wei-ch'i, encirclements deriving from interrelations of force form the foundations for strategy of conflict. Victory hinges on superior perception and manipulation of this pattern.[32]

The final stage of the Chinese Communist offensive was

annihilation, as in wei-ch'i it is the capture or killing of a hostile group. Somewhat in opposition to the maxim of Sun Tzu, the Chinese military theorist of the (estimated) fourth century B.C., which directs a general never to press his opponent too hard, the Communists never voluntarily permitted an encircled enemy group to escape. In general, capture was facilitated by exploitation of psychological encirclement frequently deriving from and based upon the effects of its physical counterpart: the sense of isolation and of hopelessness which inevitably pervades an encircled unit. In revolutionary war as in wei-ch'i, encirclement is the most effective method of annihilation.

Implementing this general model of tri-stage offensive, the Chinese Communists stressed ten theoretical maxims of operational strategy. Although not all of these principles can be naturally and usefully likened to wei-ch'i methods, the majority are illuminated when compared to the strategic principles of the game. The complete set of ten postulates, as formulated by Mao Tse-tung in 1947, is reproduced in Table III.[33]

TABLE III

MAO'S PRINCIPLES OF OPERATION

1. Attack dispersed, isolated enemy forces first; attack concentrated, strong enemy forces later.
2. Take small and medium cities and extensive rural areas first; take big cities later.
3. Make wiping out the enemy's effective strength our main objective; do not make holding or seizing a city or place our main objective. Holding or seizing a city or place is the outcome of wiping out the enemy's effective strength, and often a city or place can be held or seized for good only after it has changed hands a number of times.

4. In every battle, concentrate an absolutely superior force (two, three, four and sometimes even five or six times the enemy's strength), encircle the enemy forces completely, strive to wipe them out thoroughly and do not let any escape from the net. In special circumstances, use the method of dealing the enemy crushing blows, that is, concentrate all our strength to make a frontal attack and an attack on one or both of his flanks, with the aim of wiping out one part and routing another so that our army can swiftly move its troops to smash other enemy forces. Strive to avoid battles of attrition in which we lose more than we gain or only break even. In this way, although inferior as a whole (in terms of numbers), we shall be absolutely superior in every part and every specific campaign, and this ensures victory in the campaign. As time goes on, we shall become superior as a whole and eventually wipe out all the enemy.

5. Fight no battle unprepared, fight no battle you are not sure of winning; make every effort to be well prepared for each battle, make every effort to ensure victory in the given set of conditions as between the enemy and ourselves.

6. Give full play to our style of fighting—courage in battle, no fear of sacrifice, no fear of fatigue, and continuous fighting (that is, fighting successive battles in a short time without rest).

7. Strive to wipe out the enemy when he is on the move. At the same time, pay attention to the tactics of positional attack and capture enemy fortified points and cities.

8. With regard to attacking cities, resolutely seize all enemy fortified points and cities which are weakly defended. At opportune moments, seize all enemy fortified points and cities defended with moderate strength, provided circumstances permit. As for strongly defended enemy fortified points and cities, wait till conditions are ripe and then take them.

9. Replenish our strength with all the arms and most of the personnel captured from the enemy. Our army's main sources of manpower and *matériel* are at the front.

10. Make good use of the intervals between campaigns to rest, train and consolidate our troops. Periods of rest, training and consolidation should not in general be very long, and the enemy should so far as possible be permitted no breathing space.

Following the philosophy of historical inquiry observed in previous sections, no attempt will be made to force a wei-ch'i interpretation on every aspect of every principle of Mao's enumeration. Only the most natural and fundamental parallels will be drawn, while maintaining a consistent strategic—as opposed to tactical—point of view.

Principle 1 constitutes one of two possible answers to a recurring problem in military history: the dilemma as to which target a military commander should strike first, the enemy's outlying supplementary forces or his concentrated central position. The solution to the comparable problem in wei-ch'i theory follows the Chinese Communist line: weak groups should be attacked before strong ones. In both the revolutionary strategy of Mao Tse-tung and wei-ch'i, the decision to attack weakness before strength derives from the intensely methodical character of both conflict theories. If strong groups are attacked before weak ones, it is reasoned, the weak forces *acting in conjunction* with the strong may be able to contribute significantly to a successful over-all defense. If weak forces are neutralized first, however, they are eliminated as potential reinforcements and diversionary elements, and the strong, erstwhile unapproachable group can be attacked with maximum chance of success. The logic of this military principle underlies all Chinese Communist conflict theory and has remained pivotal in Communist international strategy since national victory in 1949–50.

Principle 2, like principle 8, is essentially a specification or development of the logic of principle 1. Its wei-ch'i meaning is comparable to that of the united front: movement toward the center of the board when the situation in the middle game is sufficiently developed. The details of edge-center theory have already been treated.

Principle 3 might, at first, seem to be deficient, or even anti-wei-ch'i, strategy in its apparent orientation toward inversion of the relative importance of the primary (territorial) and secondary (capture) objectives. In practice, however, no contradiction develops. In wei-ch'i, too, no intersection is *of itself* worth more than any other, and hence control of no *specific* intersection—city or place—is a valid objective. The Communists, in their conscious abandonment of *Schwerpunkte,* did not reject control of territory as such; rather, they objected to allowing any particular element or atom of territory to acquire value out of proportion to its physical magnitude. The second statement of the principle, moreover, is almost pure wei-ch'i: in wei-ch'i, and especially in the middle or end game, capture of hostile stones and groups generally implies seizure as territory of the intersections upon which those stones and groups stand; and, as the position develops in complexity and saturation, such action is frequently the only method of significantly expanding zones of territorial control. Regarding the final clause of 3—"often a city or place can be held or seized for good only after it has changed hands a number of times"—it is relevant to note the following statement in an exposition of wei-ch'i: "In some cases territories will change hands several times during the game and points may be occupied successively by white, by black and again by white stones." [34]

Principle 4 is possibly the key dictum of the entire set, and certainly the one to which Western analysts are most often attracted as occupying a pivotal position in Chinese Communist strategy. From the point of view of wei-ch'i, however, it is unfortunate that most analysts fail to focus on "encirclement" rather than upon "concentration," or "annihilation." Here is a concrete example of how wei-ch'i perspective may lend structure to a strategic analysis: from a wei-ch'i viewpoint, encirclement is the essence of the complexities of principle 4. Seen in this light, concentration is merely the necessary precondition for encirclement; annihilation, its logical culmination. In wei-ch'i as in war, encirclement demands superiority. It is, of course, possible to construct freak examples in which a White group encircles and captures a Black group five times its size; but, in general, starting with the four-to-one encirclement ratio needed for capture of a single stone not tangent to the edge, we can say that the margins of superiority postulated in 4 are on the order of their wei-ch'i counterparts.[35] Such strength ratios are seldom as categorically demanded by commanders in non-Communist war as by Chinese Communist generals, nor are they inherent in the rule-structure of board games other than wei-ch'i.

Principle 5 seems, on the surface, tautologous: when does a rational commander commit forces to a battle he knows he will lose? The uniqueness of Mao's dictum is probably to be found in the rigid emphasis on certainty. While 5 is by no means confined to possible analogues to wei-ch'i, a new similarity between game and revolution here emerges. In wei-ch'i, owing to the inability of stones to move unless *re*moved when captured, forces once committed to battle cannot be uncommitted and, if the battle is lost, have no hope of extrication. Hence every stone wrongly committed is a double loss: a loss of the point of territory on which it stood, and a loss because of its capture by the enemy. Similar considerations guided Chinese Communist decision-makers to stress the rule of prudent commitment in revolutionary warfare: a lightly-equipped unit, once engaged against an enemy possessing heavy weapons and with more in reserve, must either conquer, and conquer quickly, or be annihilated.[36]

Principles 6 and 10 stress the problem of timing and of effort. Although subject to several complementary wei-ch'i evaluations, only one parallel is important enough to be mentioned here: the concept of the continuous pressing of the advantage. This principle, it should be noted, runs counter to that famous law of Clausewitz which postulates the diminishing force of the attack. The principle of continuous assault is, however, good wei-ch'i: in that game, as Western players have often noted, capture of one group makes vulnerable a second, whose killing exposes a third, and so on in a cascade effect familiar to the servomechanism engineer.[37] This effect is, of course, not unique to wei-ch'i; but we are less interested in specific proofs of uniqueness than in the over-all orientation and emphasis of strategic systems. It is, therefore, significant that the Chinese Communists during the civil war both sought to exploit and realized results from this principle of constant assault in strategic, operational, and tactical maneuvers. In particular, we may note a frequent phenomenon of the civil war: surrender by a given Nationalist commander or his army, combined with constant Communist physical and psychological pressure, resulted in additional capitulation of a series of other Nationalist forces.

To a world long contemptuous of the Chinese soldier, the crumbling of the Western-armed Nationalists before the "peasant" Communists came as a shock. With the single-minded determination of those who deem themselves duped, the search was for a scapegoat. That behind Chinese Communist victory in the 1945–49 civil war and the Marxist-Leninist ideology which accompanied that victory lay an ordered yet flexible—and largely indigenous—system of thought which could be implemented to gain military success was far from Western imagination. If indeed wei-ch'i is a key to Chinese Communist revolutionary behavior, the principles of that behavior must be subject not to simplistic interpretation congealed in haste, but to the theorems of a coherent logic.

●

SIX

RETROSPECT AND PREVIEW

In the three preceding chapters the wei-ch'i model suggested in the introduction has been empirically developed and tested by application to the historical archetype of Chinese Communist insurgent strategy. Two general questions now emerge: first, whether or not the model provides a useful tool in understanding the dynamics of the Chinese Communist rise to power; second, whether or not the wei-ch'i analogy may be extended in application to the international and insurgent strategy of the Chinese Communists and their disciples on the world board.

THE HISTORICAL VALIDITY OF THE WEI-CH'I HYPOTHESIS

No theoretical model of any historical event or sequence of events is perfect. Application of the wei-ch'i analogy to certain aspects of modern Chinese historical reality should, therefore, not be evaluated by criteria of absolute validity or invalidity. On the contrary, the analogy is governed by a multi-valued logic: the *degree* of its correctness depends upon the *degree* of correspondence between the distinctive principles and patterns of the game of wei-ch'i on the one hand, and of Chinese Communist warfare as formulated and implemented by Mao Tse-tung and his associates on the other. It is therefore fitting that we summarize, at least partially, the inductive evidence for accepting the wei-ch'i analogy.

The following enumeration represents a condensation of the analysis of the past three chapters. With the potential extension of the model to insurgencies other than the Chinese in mind, our language is as general as possible.[1]

In *structural characteristics,* the Maoist version of revolutionary war is comparable to wei-ch'i in respect to time and space.

> *One:* both are protracted struggles of slow but gradually increasing tempo.
>
> *Two:* Maoist warfare profits by, and wei-ch'i provides, an extensive theater of operations.[2]
>
> *Three:* for both, the extent of the theater combined with the slowness of play permits dispersion of strategic forces in discontinuous arrangements.

In *development of patterns of force,* Maoist revolution is comparable to handicap wei-ch'i.

> *Four:* at the outset of the conflict, the insurgent is in substantially the position of a player *without* a handicap in that he lacks actual power

(stones and influence) but has potential power (possession of certain capabilities to develop forces and influence).[3]

Five: at the outset of the conflict, the counterinsurgent is substantially in the position of a player *with* a handicap in that he possesses a limited amount of both actual and potential power; further, his handicap (actual) power tends, like Black's handicap in wei-ch'i, to be oriented to the center of the board with respect to the influence which it disseminates.[4]

Six: the initial phase of the insurgency is characterized by the same fluidity that is prevalent in the wei-ch'i opening, with both sides having similar dispersion of force.

Seven: the intermediate phase of the insurgency is characterized by a war of jigsaw pattern comparable to the conflict of encirclement and counterencirclement in the wei-ch'i middle game.

Eight: the terminal phase of the insurgency is characterized, if the strategic ability differential of the players is significantly in favor of the insurgent, by resolution of the pattern in his favor, just as near the end of a wei-ch'i game between two similarly unequal players.

In *strategic objectives,* Maoist warfare is comparable to wei-ch'i.

Nine: throughout the insurgency, the principal military and political objectives of the insurgent are maximization of his control over the human- and geographic-level boards, just as in wei-ch'i the (primary) objective of the player is to maximize control over the wei-ch'i board.

Ten: throughout the insurgency, the secondary (and often intervening) objective of the insurgent is annihilation of hostile military and political forces (and concomitant preservation of his own), just as in wei-ch'i the secondary (and often intervening) aim is capture of hostile groups (and concomitant defense of his own).

In *territory-making policies and techniques,* Maoist revolution is comparable to wei-ch'i with respect to the strategic attainment of primary objectives.

Eleven: throughout the insurgency, the political strategy of Maoist revolution demands that primary attention be given to gaining the active and organized support of peasants on the periphery of the society and, though only secondarily, of other classes. Thus the insurgent seeks, like a good wei-ch'i player, to develop territory primarily along the edges of the board and only secondarily in the center:

(a) because the primary objective (for the insurgent, the peasants; for the wei-ch'i player, the edge intersections) is quantitatively more significant than any other portion of the theater of operations.

(b) because the objective can be obtained

157

(influenced) with the smallest cost/effectiveness input-output ratio.

(Primary allocation of resources to the edge, however, should not prevent attempts to maximize influence over the entire theater.)

Twelve: insurgent strategy calls for early domination of the hinterland and formation of countryside base areas, with secondary—and considerably later—emphasis on plains and urban areas. The insurgent, like the good wei-ch'i player, plays first in the corners, then along the sides, and finally extends toward the center.

In *strategies pertaining to base areas,* Maoist revolution is comparable to wei-ch'i.

Thirteen: patterns of consolidation of base areas are comparable to those in wei-ch'i formation of territory: first, loose approximate control with a few stones and reduction of hostile influence; then, tightening with many stones in a saturation pattern. On the military level, this development constitutes the evolution of guerrilla warfare; on the political level, psychological encirclement.

Fourteen: strategy used by the insurgent to counter attacks on base areas is comparable to wei-ch'i defense of positions:

(a) when the insurgent/counterinsurgent strength ratio is small (as is frequently the case, especially in the early phases), insurgent strategy requires flexibility to permit withdrawal, sacrifice, or even abandonment of ground, preferably followed by an encircling counterattack if feasible, just as, in an unconsolidated situation, wei-ch'i demands similar adaptability.

(b)   when the insurgent/counterinsurgent strength ratio is large, insurgent strategy prescribes an engagement on the perimeter of, or even outside, the base area, just as a wei-ch'i player prevents inroads on a well-consolidated position.

Finally, *in strategies for destruction of hostile forces*, Maoist warfare is comparable to wei-ch'i.

Fifteen: in revolutionary war, as in wei-ch'i, "killing" in the wei-ch'i sense—without actual annihilation—is a characteristic theme. Forces (stones) thus immobilized are ultimately surrendered (taken up at the end of the game).

Sixteen: both in the military strategy of insurgency and in wei-ch'i, decision is reached by encirclement and capture of hostile forces in a three-stage pattern (common to grand strategy, operations, and tactics):

(a)   isolation or disconnection of enemy forces from reinforcements and bases.

(b)   formation of an encirclement force around enemy forces combined, if possible, with encirclement from within (subversion, infiltration, guerrilla operations in the enemy's rear).

(c)   annihilation after completion of the encirclement.

159

Seventeen: political techniques of insurgency, directed against the enemy, correspond to the structure of wei-ch'i capture: subversion, propaganda, *noyautage,* and so forth are all wei-ch'i techniques of "negative" psychological encirclement corresponding to and complementing physical isolation on the military level.

As earlier indicated, these seventeen points do not constitute the totality of the evidence validating the wei-ch'i model of Chinese Communist insurgent strategy. In addition to these crude and general similarities, many more subtle points of resemblance may be found. One, for example, lies in the possible similarity between the Maoist theory of initiative in war and the wei-ch'i concept of *hsien-shou:* both stress possible conservation of the initiative while on the defensive, and by what even seems to be defensive action, in contrast to the offensive-oriented Western interpretation of initiative.[5]

Another resemblance relates to sacrifice. In almost every game of wei-ch'i, there are countless minor sacrifices, as in permitting a stone, or even several stones, to be killed or captured as a unit force judged unworthy of preservation.[6] Chinese Communist commanders have likewise been known to commit stones (men) to a diversionary attack deemed strategically necessary, even though the deployment will certainly result in the unit's destruction. In contrast to wei-ch'i sacrifice, chess sacrifice seldom occurs and, when it does, if deliberate and successful, is considered evidence of consummate skill. Western moral indignation at Asian sacrifice in war—and, for that matter, in situations more pacific—may be merely indicative of the difference between the two strategic value systems.

Despite the incompleteness of our enumeration of similarities, enough evidence is at hand to draw specific conclusions with regard to the relation between the Chinese Communist system of revolution and the game of wei-ch'i.

As this summary shows, the constellation of features customarily understood by Western analysts to define Maoist revolution—protraction, base areas, popular support, and so forth—can be successfully paralleled with characteristic aspects of wei-ch'i strategy. As a result, it is apparent that similarities between correct Chinese Communist strategy and correct wei-ch'i strategy are deep: far deeper, we would predict, than are similarities between *any* two effective strategies of conflict founded only on the common recognition of such universal strategic excellences as efficiency, mobility, security, or surprise.[7] For example, wei-ch'i would prove an artificial analogue to American or British strategy in the American War of Independence, to Allied strategy in the 1944 campaign in France, or even to Soviet partisan strategy behind German lines in 1941–45.[8] Inspection will show that each of these conflicts lacked one, and usually more, of the critical characteristics specified in the seventeen points above.

Upon the basis of the crude inductive evidence presented earlier in this section, it is possible to distinguish three ways in which the wei-ch'i model can improve our understanding of Chinese Communist insurgent strategy: explanation; illustration; and generalization.

Wei-ch'i provides a useful tool for explaining the often paradoxical principles of Chinese Communist insurgent doctrine. In the Introduction, certain problems were listed as illustrative examples: emphasis by the Chinese Communists on formation of base areas and, at the same time, on strategic mobility; insistence on protracted war and also on efficient operations of quick decision; desire to maximize complexity of pattern and to manipulate that complexity to revolutionary advantage, in contrast to the generally accepted dictum of Western military strategy that effective strategic style is simple.

The first paradox has caused much confusion among students of and experts on Chinese Communist strategy. Two general, if contradictory, interpretations have been suggested: that the true principle is territory and that, accordingly, Chinese Communist strategy is similar to that advocated by the French military theorist Jomini in the early nineteenth century in its extreme emphasis on the base of operations; that the true principle of the system is absolute flexibility demanding rejection of all responsibilities and requirements of territorial control. A realistic, integrated solution can be found by application of wei-ch'i theory. In wei-ch'i, a player need not control a given intersection but must seek to control the *maximum* number of intersections. If strategic points—or the holding of a specific place—conflict with territorial control in the maximal sense, strategy must be sufficiently flexible to accept a certain loss in avoidance of a greater loss and in expectation of possible greater gain. In terms of insurgency, the Chinese Communists have never felt responsible for control of a given point on the geographic board because—not although—their objective is control of the greatest possible portion of the theater.

Because of its extensive elucidation in the writings of Mao Tse-tung and of other Chinese Communist leaders, the second paradox—quick-decision attacks in a protracted war—is better understood in the West than is the first one. In this case, too, however, wei-ch'i may be of use in demonstrating the theorem. In the early phase of a handicap wei-ch'i game, it is disadvantageous for a player without a handicap (as the Chinese Communists) to concentrate his stones in a protracted engagement, or in a series of protracted engagements, with his opponent. Given even moderately correct play on the part of his adversary, he can at best expect only a tactical stand-off—the division of a corner, or other indecisive result. Because of the initial strategic superiority, however, the tactical stalemate will only serve to increase the opponent's strategic advantage by tactically consolidating that advantage. As a result, the non-handicap player should refrain from protracted engagements until the game is well advanced and should gradually undermine his opponent's over-all advantage by placing stones in dispersed positions and attacking only briefly in any one sector. Only in this way can a player without a handicap capitalize on superior methods of play to collapse the strategic paper tiger which is his foe.

The wei-ch'i interpretation of the final paradox, that of jigsaw strategy, may be seen as corollary to the theory of quick-decision attacks by the no-handicap side: in order to reduce most effectively the opponent's initial positional superiority, operations should be conducted so that regions in which the opponent has tactical superiority become divided and encircled and cannot effectivly recombine to produce a concrete strategic advantage. Furthermore, it is evident that in wei-ch'i, as in other games, a beginner functions with progressively less efficiency the more complex becomes the situation which confronts him and, in any case, tends to oversimplify its structure. Consequently, the intricacy of strategic pattern acts as an advantage for the more experienced side. (See Map 14 for differing perceptions of pattern in a Southeast Asian war.)

Related to the explanatory role of wei-ch'i is its illustrative function. The wei-ch'i analogy is a type of model still rare in the social sciences: flexible yet formalistic. On the one hand, because it is not bound by the restrictions of the axiom-theorem method or by the ability of mathematicians to integrate a differential equation, wei-ch'i analysis of a

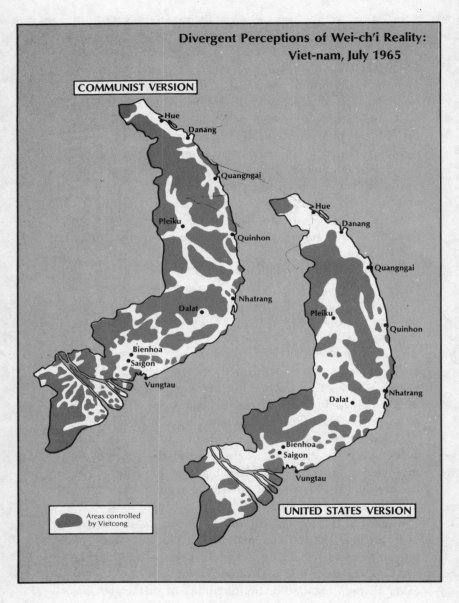

Divergent Perceptions of Wei-ch'i Reality: Viet-nam, July 1965

COMMUNIST VERSION

Hue
Danang
Quangngai
Pleiku
Quinhon
Nhatrang
Dalat
Bienhoa
Saigon
Vungtau

Hue
Danang
Quangngai
Pleiku
Quinhon
Nhatrang
Dalat
Bienhoa
Saigon
Vungtau

Areas controlled
by Vietcong

UNITED STATES VERSION

MAP 14

strategic system can go far beyond the limits of present-day, or even potentially obtainable, social science formalism. At the same time, wei-ch'i provides what might be termed the most important single feature of the formalist approach: a logical and consistent *point of view* from which to analyze one facet of Chinese civilization and decision-making. These dual characteristics contribute to the significance of wei-ch'i as a simple, efficient, and accurate simulation model of specific motifs of ·Chinese Communist insurgent warfare. In short, wei-ch'i provides a method whereby the abstract and lifeless theories propounded and repeated *ad nauseam* in Mao Tse-tung's *Selected Works,* as well as in Western historical expositions—often equally tedious—of the Chinese revolution, can be revivified and experimented with by the analysts. Particularly important in this respect is the iconic structure of wei-ch'i which maximizes the game's comprehensibility in a manner similar to the game-theory outcome matrix or the analytic approach of input-output economics.[9] The pedagogical and laboratory functions of wei-ch'i should not be underrated.

Finally, perhaps most importantly, wei-ch'i helps to determine and generalize the internal structure and logic of Chinese Communist insurgent doctrine. Most analyses have merely set forth its precepts: wei-ch'i provides one method of integrating those precepts into a coherent and ordered system. It is also a tool for the analysis of the hidden internal structure as well as of the suppressed premises of Chinese Communist insurgent strategy: a system of analogic logic. In particular, use of wei-ch'i may be expected to show that both the military and the political aspects of Chinese Communist insurgent theory derive from a single, abstract psychological concept of conflict.[10] Certainly, our use of wei-ch'i analysis uncovers notable similarity between the rationale and the structure of the strategy of forming countryside base areas and that of winning the support of the peasant classes; between certain aspects of Chinese Communist encirclement operations in warfare and the psychological foundations of Chinese Communist methods of social engineering. If the various forms of conflict—military, political, and psychological—used by the Chinese Communists in their rise to power are regulated by a single internal *Weltanschauung* mirrored in wei-ch'i, it may be possible to untangle the component of Chineseness from the component of Marxist-Leninism which went into the historical evolution of the Chinese brand of communism.

EXTENDED APPLICATION OF THE MODEL

The preceding section summarizes the case for the use of wei-ch'i as an analogic tool in the study of Chinese Communist strategy as applied in China in the years 1927 to 1949. Application of the game in the analysis of past events should not, however, preclude its use in the investigation of more recent and policy-relevant instances of Communist strategy.[11] By analogic logic, the game should be able to provide a formal methodology for elucidation of whatever post-insurgent revolutionary patterns Peking has exported to influence the conduct of international politics. Moreover, if only because of the continuity stressed by the leaders in Peking between Maoist strategy of revolution and Maoist strategy of government, wei-ch'i may furnish clues to future Chinese Communist international behavior.

A word of caution, however, is in order. Given the present state of Western knowledge of the Chinese Communist strategic system, and of Communist China in general, no definite conclusion may be drawn as to the possibility of conscious and explicit use of wei-ch'i methods either by the

Chinese Communists or by their strategic disciples. While evidence for the affirmative conclusion, at least for the Chinese case, might be drawn from several passages of Mao Tse-tung's *Selected Works,* the several passages quoted in the Introduction do not suffice to decide the question or even to weight the probabilities toward conscious employment. Substantiation of wei-chi's heuristic function must, therefore, be derived from the more indirect sources of hypothesis and experimentation.

Three fundamental axioms of the Chinese Communist approach to problem-solving, equally applicable to international diplomacy or to revolutionary warfare, come to mind. The most important of these is the territory-oriented strategic concept of Maoist politico-military doctrine.[12] The second concerns the discontinuous pattern of politico-military operations in space and time. The third, centering around operational method, involves the decisive character of disconnection, encirclement, and related wei-ch'i motifs.

The chief goal of the Chinese Communist strategy is control of territory, whether geographical or psychological. Despite the importance of operations which are aggressive and offensive, it is the territory gained, not capture per se, which, in the Communist lexicon, marks the difference between victory and defeat. In short, the desideratum is ultimate control of space rather than immediate seizure of any given point in space. This wei-ch'i-based philosophy of conflict is one which the Westerner finds difficult to grasp. His impulse is to contain and capture his opponent's forces at the expense of forming secure bases for his own groups. His weakness is failure to recognize that another approach to conflict may deem territory-making, in the critical opening phase of operations, more profitable than capture, and more than half the payoff of offensive action. The aim of Maoist strategy from the beginning of a conflict is to pursue a course which will maximize the amount of territory encircled at the furthest point in the foreseeable future.

This fundamental concept of territory is reflected on two basic levels at which Maoist strategy may be applied: on that of geopolitical behavior, that is, in Peking's international strategy; and on that of politico-military operations in an insurgency whose conduct is influenced by the Chinese model.[13]

On the geopolitical level, the Chinese Communists may be expected to view the game in which they are engaged as free from time-bound limitations, as one in which they may set the tempo of play. The behavior of the Chinese Communists has consistently indicated that, as far as they are concerned, the opening of the international game has barely begun. Ensconced on the edge of the world board, they appear both unwilling to precipitate their presence into the center at such an early stage and willing to permit the opponent, in whatever manifestation, to make random and, from the wei-ch'i viewpoint, often wasteful plays directly proximate to the wei-ch'i territory which is the Chinese mainland.

At the same time, the Chinese Communists have by no means evinced a passive approach to the board they edge. They early placed certain diplomatic stones on intersections which appeared potentially valuable for—at minimum, psychological—territory-making; they added others; they even abandoned some as dead—in Ghana, Pakistan, and Indonesia. Further, they gave attention to certain subboards which might eventually serve as territorial regions to be joined in encirclement of the opponent. If Chinese Communists plays of this nature seemed tentative, it must be remembered that, in the wei-ch'i context, time is long and the grid is large.

It is in connection with these sub-boards that prospective Chinese Communist geopolitical strategy may best be assessed. Major targets for that strategy, with its wei-ch'i concepts, are the developing nations and their populaces. In particular, the populace of a developing nation satisfies the Chinese Communist criterion that, in the opening and the middle of a conflict, the most economical play is to influence the socio-economic periphery. The correctness of this assessment of cost-effectiveness is buttressed by knowledge of the proclivity of the Western powers to concentrate play in the center of the world board. The philosophical basis of whatever territorization the Chinese Communists attempt in the developing nations will remain belief in the wei-ch'i axiom: "As the edge goes, so goes the board."

In the context of insurgency within a single nation, Maoist doctrine is effectively identical to that just sketched. The aim is maximum territory both in geographic area and in popular support. As the Chinese Communists learned from experience, the military control of extensive regions of the countryside and the political cooperation—organized and active—of the broad masses of the people are indivisible in ensuring permanency of territorial control. Only such geographic and human bases provide the insurgent with the security with which to meet counterinsurgent operations and, ultimately, to begin a counteroffensive: "If we lose the field, we cannot hold the town." [14] If there seems for some time to come, or ever, little chance of actual Chinese-directed implementation of this insurgency theory on the far reaches of the world board, there will still be opportunity for export of military advice and military advisers to propagate and implement the theme.

Behind the desire of Maoist strategists for territory maximization, whether by geopolitical or military means, lies a typically wei-ch'i flexibility. In keeping with this concept, the Chinese Communists see no need, in their world game, to continue operations which, despite the original estimate and perhaps through changes over which they have no control, do not promise significant gain. Their philosophy frees them to abandon the unprofitable and to play elsewhere. In particular, if the opponent is concentrating his efforts to make one part of the board his strategic territory, the Chinese Communists will then play throughout the remainder of the board, thereby gaining strategic advance at the price of what appears to be localized defeat. Such action may lose some of its efficacy if the territory abandoned is qualitatively important. But the long-term character of the game the Chinese Communists play contributes to the possibility that what is today qualitatively important may, another day, be valueless. By their flexibility, the Communists may even —and deliberately—contribute to the devaluation. What is important to them is the number of stones, the quantity of intersections held at game's end.

In insurgent military operations also, Chinese Communist strategy demands unconditional flexibility. Flexibility is, to be sure, a recognized cardinal virtue in any rational military system. The two major principles of war enunciated by Marshal Foch were economy and flexibility. In military practice in the West, flexibility has varying operational significance in different strategic systems: the flexibility in American-Indian tactics against white settlers cannot be unconditionally identified with that of the German blitzkrieg in France in 1940. Chinese Communist flexibility revolves around wei-ch'i-derived rejection of strategic points except as they contribute to territory maximization. In other words, strategic points have special value only as a result of the interrelation of forces on the board. As in wei-ch'i, every point is a priori of equal value until its relevancy is determined by its expected contribution to territorization. Pragmatically, the Chinese Communists believe that control of no point should be contested more than the territorial pay-off warrants.

The second fundamental wei-ch'i principle underlying Chinese Communist strategy, both pure and derived, geopolitical and insurgent, is related to, but not identical with, the territorial concept just discussed. It concerns the jigsaw pattern of the conflict—the discontinuity of the loci of force of whichever side. This concept may also be formulated as the principle of maximal dispersion.

It has been a tenet of the majority of strategic theorists and military writers, Western and Chinese, that military success depends upon concentration of resources at some decisive point. Represented in extreme form by Clausewitz and Jomini, this notion is also basic to the conceptual schemes of such diverse times and cultures as those represented by Sun Tzu and Liddell Hart: the exhortation of the Chinese military work, the *Sun-Tzu ping-fa* (*Sun Tzu On War*), that "Troops [should] be thrown against the enemy as a grindstone against eggs" is mirrored in the surety of the British scholar that "The principles of war, not merely one principle, can be condensed into a single word—'concentration'." [15]

In contrast, Chinese Communist revolutionary strategy, paralleling wei-ch'i, explicitly does not depend upon concentration of force at any single point, or even at any single set of points, as a means to strategic victory. Instead, on both the geopolitical and insurgent levels of conflict, the Chinese Communists seek to attain decisive strategic advantage by exploitation of the strength of dispersed forces.

To be sure, revolutionary strategy involves varying degrees of *tactical* concentration at a *tactically* decisive point. Moreover, tactical success can, on occasion, lead to strategic success. But there is relevancy to Takagawa's pluralization of the word "point" in his title *The Vital Points of Go*. The Chinese Communists, for tactical success, pluralize by strategic dispersion: the vital strategic *points* of a specific situation will be scattered across the board of operations.

Such radical departure from classical strategic analysis requires momentary return to wei-ch'i. In that game, the principle of dispersion derives directly from the territorial concept: because each side wishes to maximize its own territory and to minimize that of its opponent, both adversaries seek constantly to invade each other's sphere of influence and, ignoring continuity of deployment, to commit forces wherever opportunity warrants. As a result, early in the game a pattern of scattered and apparently un-co-ordinated groups is created in a disposition which seems, to the unwarned strategic analyst, indicative of strategic weakness. As the game develops, however, all these dispersed forces will be seen to have a co-ordinated purpose; and the majority, to constitute bases for powerful territories. Seldom, before the final moves of the game—or even until its end, when dead stones are removed—does the pattern of force and territory become obvious to the uninstructed. In this connection, assumption at any given time by Westerners that the Chinese Communists are inactive on the world board may be more indicative of Western ignorance than of Chinese Communist frustration.

On the geopolitical level, the Chinese Communists may be expected to perceive and to manipulate the game of world politics in terms of wei-ch'i dispersion. Knowing that concentration is not a necessary precondition for strategic value, they will not think in terms of lavish commitments: the influence generated by three stones may be no greater than that generated by one. Strategy rather than stringency will dictate what to an affluent nation like the United States would seem a miniscule outlay of economic, military, and other aid. Yet because of the calculation which determines the dispersal, the return in the form of Chinese Communist influence may be considerable. To paraphrase a remark in Chapter I, force is far less important than the disposition of that force.

In the dispersal of diplomatic and political stones throughout the world, the Chinese Communists are supported by the wei-ch'i view of protracted conflict. They believe that the stones they place with care and economy will—in time —develop, increase, and unite, not in a direct or simple way —such as a continent's "going Chinese"—but in a more subtle, insidious pattern.[16] Some will undoubtedly be reduced or eliminated, but it is axiomatic to Chinese Communist strategy that, as in wei-ch'i, though individual stones may be captured, it will be at the price of letting other stones survive and propagate. Nor are the Chinese Communists unduly anxious that, among the stones which flourish, there necessarily be some in regions proximate to their largest territory, mainland China. Nearness, by Chinese Communist philosophy, is not synonymous with influence. In fact, areas where conflict has not yet developed serve Communist purposes best, giving as they do fair field for geopolitical expansion. Concomitantly, the Communists cannot be expected to be impressed by play against their borders—as long as it does not transgress them. Not only is the flexibility, to return to that concept, of the opponent positionally limited, but also the Communists are in no way deterred from playing stones at will behind the line deliberately designed by the opponent for containment.

Once again, these concepts are mirrored in the insurgent situation. On the political level of insurgent conflict, Maoist theory seeks to implement subversion from within: infiltration and *noyautage* of non-Communist and anti-Communist organizations—military, political, economic, cultural. The

173

aim is not only defensive: advance discovery of plans so that counteraction can be taken; erosion of contrary convictions; destruction of morale. It is also offensive. The objective is to make no region of the human board controlled by the opponent safe for him; to press him on every side; and, if he persists in his presence, to force him to an exaggerated effort in attempts at keeping control.

On the geographic level, whenever feasible, the Chinese Communists will also exploit calculated discontinuity by dispersion of initially small insurgent forces to "arouse the masses" and to develop military territory. The principle can almost be formulated mathematically as an instance of the nonadditivity of military force: in Chinese Communist warfare, a thousand units of fifty men are sometimes worth more than fifty units of a thousand men. The wei-ch'i-type logic behind this deliberate dispersion and division of force finds expression in the words of Sun Tzu:

> The enemy must not know where I intend to give battle. For if he does not know where I intend to give battle he must prepare in a great many places. And when he prepares in a great many places, those I have to fight in any one place will be few.[17]

The ultimate challenge of the motif of discontinuity of force lies in its effectiveness in forcing the counterinsurgent to disperse his own forces—but in a defensive manner and for a defensive purpose. In wei-ch'i, voluntary dispersion with the aim of encirclement or territory is necessary and laudable; however, dispersion for containment of the opponent's dispersion is considered futile and dangerous. As long as a counterinsurgent feels it his responsibility to maintain authority in a given region, dispersion for defense becomes unavoidable. The spirit of the problem is accurately, if unconsciously, caught in a formulation by a French general:

> Turning to the geographic aspect, a choice must be made of those areas which we wish either to defend or to threaten or to attack. This choice will therefore be concerned on the one hand with those areas which protect points vital to us, on the other with those which threaten the enemy's vulnerable points, and if possible those in which action would be comparatively easy. We should try to choose areas which can form bases for further action (e.g. Cuba). We should not allow ourselves to be drawn into areas where the enemy can deploy considerable effort at little cost to himself while we are forced to expend resources on a large scale (e.g. South East Asia).[18]

We turn finally to the third axiom which governs Chinese Communist strategy on the world board. Guided by the concept of territorization and relying upon the principle of discontinuity of effort, Peking envisions three interrelated strategic phases in the disintegration of any power which they identify as enemy: the phase of isolation or disconnection; the phase of encirclement; and the phase of annihilation.

The phase of disconnection depends not only on the physical disconnection of anti-Chinese zones by means of neutral or pro-Chinese zones but also upon the psychological disconnection and isolation of enemy or pro-enemy groups in the world arena.[19] The tactics employed will be diverse and sometimes contradictory to Chinese professions for other purposes. For instance, the notion of racism is a tactic designed to isolate. Encouragement of religious factionalism is another. Or there may be attempts at fragmenting, by what amounts to psychological disconnection, a coalition of pro-enemy politico-military stones. Again, complex pressures—military, political, diplomatic, economic, cultural—may be brought to bear on nations geographically encircling a neutral or pro-enemy zone. Whatever the tactics, they reflect Chinese Communist confidence that only by the strategic dispersion of Communist force throughout many regions and on many levels of the spectrum of conflict activity can division of the enemy be effectively and universally realized.

The phase of encirclement, in the true wei-ch'i sense, is a secondary stage, growing out of and blending with that of disconnection and isolation and developing in a highly uneven pattern. The Chinese Communists know that, both in principle and in practice, encirclement can occur anywhere at any propitious time, without reference to a theoretical calendar providing for firsts, seconds, and thirds; and that it can take many forms. It may develop as diplomatic isolation; internal discontent against a ruling class; military threat on a country's borders; racial antagonisms within a nation; the co-ordinated hostility of several countries against one nation; economic embargo. The means are immaterial; the end is the immobilization by encirclement of a disconnected political or social unit.

The final phase—that of annihilation—has been picturesquely foreseen by Mao Tse-tung: ". . . a worldwide net [will be formed] from which the fascist monkeys can find no escape, our enemy will be doomed." [20] That the Chinese Communists as yet appear to be far from annihilating the enemy should furnish scant consolation to a candidate for Communist-desired extinction. They are sure that the enemy will prove an active agent in his own destruction. Unable, so the Chinese Communists believe, to see the intellectual challenge of their strategy; unendowed, the Communists are confident, with the requisite psychological flexibility to counter the strategy if they see it, the enemy will contribute to his own encirclement and thus, the Communists hope, to his ultimate annihilation.

The purpose of this work is to present the intellectual challenge of Chinese Communist strategy, not to analyze Western psychological limitations in coping with that strategy.[21] It is not inconsistent, however, to point out two particularly characteristic features of Chinese Communist encirclement/annihilation patterns derived from wei-ch'i which are at variance with Western strategic thought.

The first may be called interiority. In his lucid discussion of the wei-ch'i rules of capture, and of the terms "inside" and "outside" in connection with encirclement of hostile groups, Goodell says:

> The easiest explanation is a comparison with ancient warfare. Consider that an army occupies a walled city. An enemy may surround the outside of this city but they cannot capture the occupying army until they actually invade the territory inside the wall. There are many famous battles where enemy troops have in some way entered such a besieged city secretly and then, attacking inside and out, demolished the occupying troops.[22]

It is exactly this reliance upon encirclement from the inside which characterizes the Chinese Communist strategy of conflict on the world board. A concrete instance was the attempt by Peking during the early 1960's to develop amicable relations with Pakistan: the play of stones inside an American defense alliance (SEATO). On the level of insurgency, both infiltration-subversion by cadres within government units and development of guerrilla warfare and harassing attack within areas nominally "White" represent a similar structure of attack from within. Encirclement from the inside is one of the most insidious and at the same time one of the most sophisticated techniques of Chinese Communist insurgent warfare.

The second feature may be called indirection. This characteristic of Chinese Communist strategy has already been commented on in a purely military framework, as reflected in typically concentric rather than eccentric development of encirclement patterns.[23] In other words, rather than proceeding from a single base in the manner of envelopment, encirclement tends to take the more subtle form of co-ordinated convergence of many bases and strategic forces. Chinese Communist wei-ch'i encirclement is indirect in the sense that it is a protracted process depending heavily on interior rather than exterior line operations, and is often not apparent until its final phases. Although application of the adjective "indirect" to encirclement, itself an essentially indirect approach, might appear tautologous, it nevertheless serves to emphasize a fundamental distinction, one which goes far to explain, for example, the depressingly uniform failure of the encirclement and annihilation campaigns in the hands of South Vietnamese army commanders in their conflict with Hanoi and the contrastingly high success of Communist encirclement methods.

Interiority and indirection are, on the whole, favorable labels within the context of modern strategic fashion. They carry a connotation of Oriental subtlety as opposed to Occidental directness. In all forms of human conflict, however, and most of all in war, no single motif or pattern is unconditionally advantageous; whatever utility may derive from its use depends upon the way in which the technique is embedded in an entire system of strategic action. The wei-ch'i perspective which leads to the realization of the importance of encirclement in Chinese Communist strategy also makes possible recognition of certain tensions—perhaps even contradictions—inherent in that system.

Sun Tzu once said that an encircled enemy should be given a chance to flee the encircler, for otherwise the attacker would suffer heavy losses in a battle of attrition against a desperate foe.[24] In this proposition, the ancient thinker enunciated the all-important wei-ch'i principle of the incomplete victory. Indications in the late 1960's, however, point to total, unequivocal refusal on the part of the Chinese Communist strategic model to admit the necessity of incomplete victory in any game: world, national, or even sub-national. Discounting the unlikely contingency that this concept of complete victory is merely part of the model's verbal superstructure rather than of its internal dynamics, we have here a non-, even anti-wei-ch'i objective in the third (annihilation) phase of any conflict operation.

It is, of course, a verified fact that, if a sufficiently capable player confronts a sufficiently incompetent one on the wei-ch'i board, the chance is that the superior side will evince only a minimum of peaceful coexistence as a conflict compromise. The possibility of coexistence cannot, however, in principle be rejected; yet it is precisely the possibility of coexistence that the strategy of Mao Tse-tung in principle refuses to concede.[25] The concept of victory to which the Chinese Communist system subscribes seems inconsistent with the means of encirclement prescribed to attain victory, just as in wei-ch'i the means of capture—again encirclement —is intrinsically insufficient to achieve capture of every hostile group upon the board. Chinese Communist emphasis upon total victory, taken *in conjunction with* the over-all wei-ch'i structure of the revolutionary model, may be the factor of irrationality in an otherwise rational deductive system.

We shall not here explore the detailed policy implications of this reasoning. If, however, our evaluation is even partially valid, then a politico-military side facing an opponent using Chinese Communist doctrine should be able to exploit the inconsistency for its own positive utility. On the level of military behavior, in particular, we might postulate a very different system of counteraction from that generally accepted in recent Western military thought.

The battle of Dienbienphu, in which some twenty thousand officers and men of the French army were casualties or captured and a Western army defeated by an Asian in pitched positional warfare, has been held up to the Western world, by Communist and non-Communist alike, as the greatest defeat of Western military power on the Asian mainland. Yet, as a counterpoise to Chinese Communist warfare, the *Western strategy which conceived Dienbienphu, if not the tactics and the logistics which implemented that strategy, may have been correct.*[26] Wei-ch'i analysis would so indicate.

The argument rests upon two axioms: first, a desire or demand by the Maoist side's high command for complete victory; second, the extremely close, almost axiomatic, connection in the Maoist model between encirclement on the one hand and annihilation on the other. According to the second of these axioms, Maoist theory hypothesizes that, if encirclement is realized, annihilation must be only a small distance removed in strategic space; but *encirclement is the only creative strategic mechanism recognized by the theory and consequently, when no further encirclement is possible, the model provides no directive, and technique will be reduced to direct, frontal attack.* These corollaries of axiom two seem well documented by the case histories of the Chinese civil war and of the Korean and Indochina conflicts.[27]

To make concrete this abstract reasoning, we note first that the principle underlying the battle of Dienbienphu on the part of the French was that of placing a unit force—a stone—in a position where it could be encircled on the ground as completely as desired by the Communists. Axiom one would here come into play: the Communist command would desire total victory on the operational board. By axiom two, they would achieve, or seek to achieve, victory by encirclement of the isolated force and subsequent attacks upon its defensive perimeter. From the French standpoint, however, the encirclement would effect concentration of Communist forces as target for superior Western matériel—artillery, armor, and aircraft.

It is instructive to analyze the actual results. Contrary to French expectations, the Dienbienphu garrison was ultimately overrun and annihilated, and Communist confidence in Communist military theory must have been in no way lessened, despite fatal casualties far heavier—by a factor of three or three and one-half—than the defenders suffered.[28] French failure resulted from a complex of tactical and logistical blunders which have been emphasized for years after the event: bad positioning of the airstrip, bad planning of the deployments, insufficient helicopter support, insufficient air support in general, etc.[29]

What is the lesson? Given sufficient measure of counterinsurgent technological efficiency, given the imperfect applicability to reality—or at least to certain reality—of the postulated wei-ch'i structure of Maoist warfare, the strategic concept underlying the French approach to the battle of Dienbienphu—deliberate invitation to the insurgent to concentrate his forces in encirclement—may be valid guide to future campaigns. With proper command, organization, and tactics, casualties to the defender will be nowhere near the complete annihilation of French forces as in the Indochinese battle and may, if sufficient advanced technology is applied, be confined within an acceptable loss limit comprising only a fraction of the committed force. By thus creating a situation in which the limitations of the wei-ch'i offensive method can be exposed, the defender can cause the casualty level of the attacking insurgent—drastic enough at Dienbienphu— to exceed any rational military threshold.

Psychologically committed to total objectives, the Chinese Communists and their disciples appear trapped by the limitations of their wei-ch'i methods for achieving them. Any strategic system, the Maoist included, is but an approximation of reality; and the more closed and static the system, the greater the opportunity for the opponent to manipulate its lack of flexibility.[30] Study of wei-ch'i is key to such exploitation.

The Chinese Communist strategic system is but the latest and most publicized manifestation of over two thousand years of Chinese strategic thought. There seems little doubt that wei-ch'i, as a collateral element of the same tradition, is able to aid in the illumination of the still imperfectly understood thought of Mao Tse-tung. The degree of this illumination, however, will depend in great part upon the imagination with which the analogy constructed in the preceding chapters is elaborated. Wei-ch'i is not, and cannot be, a purely "scientific" analytic method in the study of any given aspect of war or politics. Nevertheless, it is possible to develop the general correspondences outlined in this work into more detailed analogies between the highly sophisticated and subtle strategic technology of wei-ch'i and the equally sophisticated and subtle methodology of Chinese Communist revolution. With development of detail and with flexible re-interpretation of the structure of wei-ch'i, the tools are available with which to define and to predict with some exactitude specific operational objectives and methods of Chinese Communist strategy on the world board and its subboards.

An article on cross-cultural communications once defined

"the way for telling the contingent from the necessary, the intra-cultural from the pan-human" as "the search for a perspective within which the self appears no more important than the other. . . ." [31] The argument postulated is no less applicable for strategy than for any other form of human activity. Any school of strategic thought, whether Chinese Communist or Clausewitzian, contains two intellectual elements: on the one hand, universal pan-strategic principles; on the other, axioms which are the distinguishing features of the particular system and which represent the empirical and subjective conclusions of its exponents. The function of the wei-ch'i model is to provide a systematic methodology for analyzing structuring and the contingent elements of the Chinese Communist strategic system.

The importance of this function may be illustrated by the following passages from an essay by Fung Yu-lan, one of modern China's leading philosophers. As already mentioned, the hsiang-ch'i referred to is the Chinese equivalent of Western chess; both wei-ch'i and hsiang-ch'i are generically called ch'i. Wrote Fung:

> Wei-ch'i has wei-ch'i rules; hsiang-ch'i has hsiang-ch'i rules. If one is playing wei-ch'i, then one is bound by wei-ch'i rules; and likewise for hsiang-ch'i. Nor is it necessarily a matter of choice what form of ch'i is played. Stones and the grid-board are necessary prerequisites for wei-ch'i; the chessmen and the eighty-one squares, for hsiang-ch'i.

Turning to the shortcomings of the Chinese intelligentsia of the early republican period who failed to recognize the problems of Chinese society, Fung proceeds:

> This is just like someone who only knows how to play wei-ch'i and who does not know that there is more than one kind of ch'i, who, when he sees the opening position in

183

hsiang-ch'i, cries, "How can you start like this? You're wrong, you're wrong!" Again, seeing a piece move, he criticizes, "How can you move a piece already played? You're playing illegally." When the wei-ch'i people of this world, who don't know hsiang-ch'i, criticize it in this fashion, it can truly be said to be the funniest thing in the world.[32]

The problems confronted by American and, in fact, all Western statesmen, soldiers, and scholars in dealing with the People's Republic of China or with Maoist strategy in general are precisely those of the hsiang-ch'i player faced with a wei-ch'i game and a wei-ch'i strategy. All too often the Western reaction resembles that implied by Fung Yu-lan: suspicion, confusion, and contempt. "Know yourself and know your enemy," said Sun Tzu; "one hundred battles, one hundred victories." As a means, if only partial, to knowledge of the Chinese Communist player, understanding of the protracted game is a critical adjunct for the Western side in all strategic situations of Sino-Western conflict or accord.

APPENDIX I

One unfortunate aspect of modern social science is that many theories and models are presented once in paper, article, or book and then forgotten. In the conviction that the wei-ch'i thesis of the present work does not deserve this fate, this research note is appended to the body of substantive treatment to outline suggestions for future investigation.

GOOD WEI-CH'I

As we have had frequent occasion to stress, the preceding chapters of this essay have developed only first-order approximations between wei-ch'i and Chinese Communist strategy, the majority of which are on a high level of abstraction. With knowledge of wei-ch'i encompassing only the general precepts of the strategy employed in the analogy, together with a comparable degree of tactical skill, no player could attain even the lowest grade of amateur wei-ch'i rank.

The development, extension, and elaboration of the wei-ch'i principles already described is the science—or art—of

185

higher wei-ch'i strategy. To judge by the number of persons skilled in that strategy, compared with the number who play chess on the master level, mastery of wei-ch'i is indeed difficult. One avenue of development for the wei-ch'i analogy of this book lies in extension of its propositions into this neglected realm of higher strategy.

Such extension could be realized in two major ways. First, we could orient our studies to analysis and synthesis of the mass of wei-ch'i games, openings, problems, and positions with the concomitant descriptions, evaluations, and commentaries bequeathed to the modern world by generations of Chinese and Japanese wei-ch'i thinkers.[1] In many cases, linguistic difficulties may be minimized by attention to diagramatically recorded situations and sequences of approved play rather than to the critiques, often in themselves intricate and obscure. To co-ordinate the quantities of data which Asian libraries might afford, extensive use could be made of electronic data processing: the bibliography of one recent work on wei-ch'i, for instance, contains 126 pages.[2] From the analysis of these empirical studies may come the realization of the applicability to study of Chinese Communist revolution of many aspects of wei-ch'i at present unknown, in whole or in part, in the West.

A second approach might complement the first. Since the development of modern game theory and computer technology, certain interest has been focused upon the possibility of computerized chess. A more practical and urgent task may well be the programming of a machine for wei-ch'i play.

Opinions would differ as to the difficulty of the task. Obviously, it would be possible to have a computer play a crude caricature of the game, with little more in the line of inputs than simple formalization of the principles described in Chapter I plus a large number of openings and capture patterns. Such a program, however, besides being unwieldy and ineffectual against a competent player, would negate the reason for its existence: advancing our knowledge of the decision processes which underlie higher wei-ch'i strategy. According to some sources, mathematicians have tried without avail to write such a program or formalization of the wei-ch'i mind.[3]

A brief sketch of what must be attempted may proceed from the concepts of satisficing and planning horizon set forth in a paper of Herbert Simon.[4] According to his model of rational behavior, rationality consists not of optimizing (in wei-ch'i, the theoretically optimal strategy exists in principle but is, and will remain, unknown even to the most skilled because of the number of possible variations which would have to be taken into account in computing it) but of *satisficing:* that is, looking ahead a given, limited number of moves—say five or ten—in advance and following that course of action which will maximize expected utility on this horizon. This principle requires the search for a strategy S which, employed at time t, will lead to an optimally satisfactory position at time t plus T for some interval T. This strategy might, in turn, depend upon certain weights given to such factors as territory, mobility, influence, capture, killing, self-preservation, and so on. The problem of formalization of these intuitive notions is one for the mathematician or the mathematical logician, with ultimate computerization possible.

As a final suggestion, it would be interesting to experiment, in the classical, empiricist manner and mathematically as well, with the possibility that the wei-ch'i strategy which has evolved is, in fact, nonoptimal and counterable by a different strategic approach to the game. Two general reasons for seeking such a strategy may be posited. First, the development of strategy in any game tends to be conditioned by stereotyped expectations by A that certain methods will cause the defeat of B; by B that certain other methods will, conversely, effect victory over A. In this way, a dialectical feedback situation is created according to which what has happened in the past conditions and shapes future strategy and policy. That such conditioning may lead to nonoptimal results in wei-ch'i was proven in the 1930's by Wu Ch'ing-yuan's successful abandonment of certain classical motifs of the game's strategy. Second, assuming that a variant strategy could be found for pure wei-ch'i, the discovery might have definite policy implications for counterinsurgency theory and practice, leading to a strategy for counterinsurgency which does not merely imitate insurgent practices but explicitly manipulates the insurgent's erroneous strategy for counterinsurgent payoff.

Poor Wei-ch'i

To learn chess—or wei-ch'i—it is often claimed that one must go to the master. As emphasized in the preceding section, study of the intricacies of master play is in fact one important method by which to deepen and develop the wei-ch'i analogy to Chinese Communist strategic systems. However, given the lack of Western sophistication when confronted with situations characteristic of the Asian game, it is equally relevant to make special study of the errors, misconceptions, and disorientations characteristic of beginner play. This is the study of poor wei-ch'i.

As has been indicated, in analysis of good wei-ch'i the pivotal problem is not acquisition of data but the processing of data which already exists. By contrast, analysis of poor wei-ch'i, the play of beginners, must start with the proposition that (just as in the case of chess) detailed material on the subject is seldom published. Intensive search of Western-language wei-ch'i literature has produced only one recorded game between a beginner and a competent player, precisely the type of situation relevant in counterinsurgency application.[5] Because of the focus of the literature on master play, analysis of the behavior of novices must begin with collection of information regarding the interaction of the beginner with the game, through laboratory experiments concerning the catalytic reactions produced. In particular, the following questions are pertinent:

1. What are the most common strategic and operational errors made by the uninstructed wei-ch'i novice?

2. How does the uninstructed novice dynamically adjust his behavior over time, improving his strategies and trying new ones in play with a superior (instructed) player?

3. What is the reaction of the novice to instruction, and what are the most efficient pedagogical techniques for that instruction?

4. What effect on learning ability in wei-ch'i, either instructed or uninstructed, do the characteristics of the learner have: age, intelligence, sex, experience with Asian matters (excluding Asian games), knowledge of chess, knowledge of Western military affairs, knowledge of mathematics or formal logic, etc.? (Such considerations might be relevant in education for counterinsurgency.)

Investigation of these and related problems falls within the sphere of psychology, particularly of learning theory. Past research on problems of strategic decision which makes use of the experimental methods of scientific psychology may be invoked as a guiding image.[6] The concrete results of this line of attack may then be applied to understanding and improving the responses of Western military and political leaders to the type of non-Western conflict situation postulated in the introduction to this work.

As for the specific hypotheses to be tested, the present work has only set forth certain testable propositions relating to the problem heading 1 above. In the course of the historical exposition through which we have carried the development of the wei-ch'i model, several prevalent errors have been noted as characteristic of the play of opponents of the Chinese Communists since 1927. Future analysis is likely to extend the list:

1. *Inversion of the relative importance of the objectives* of territory and annihilation: the tendency of non-Communist strategy to be enemy-oriented, emphasizing search-and-destroy rather than territory-making operations.

2. *Failure to wage protracted war,* with emphasis on time-limits, time-targets, and a psychological framework of quick decision.

3. *Over-emphasis on linearity, simplicity, continuity,* and concentration of force-deployments in unconventional war; disorientation by the failure of the insurgent to develop operations conforming to these patterns.

4. *An offensive strategy oriented to the forward thrust,* without sufficient emphasis on encirclement; or, if encirclement is attempted, failure to achieve the sophistication and efficiency characteristic of the Communist counterpart.

5. *A defensive strategy oriented to containment,* without sufficient emphasis on flexible defense-offense, retreat, and strategic mobility.

6. *Orientation toward zero- or unidimensional force,* connection with cities, railroads, strategic points, elite groups, and the like without sufficient stress on the development of the broad, two-dimensional territories fundamental to wei-ch'i.

7. *Orientation to the center of the board,* with underestimation or complete rejection of the edge as the strategic pivot of the conflict.[7]

Study of the dynamics and etiology of these deficiencies in the play of the wei-ch'i beginner may increase understanding of the attitudes which underlie their perpetuation on the politico-military board of human affairs, and of the frustrations which result.

APPENDIX II

WEI-CH'I IN WESTERN LANGUAGES:
A BIBLIOGRAPHICAL NOTE

Social science readers who wish to comprehend the un-co-ordinated, unsystematic, and bibliographically uncontrollable state of Western-language descriptions of wei-ch'i, its history and theory, have no need to visualize an abstraction: they have only to recall the situation with regard to mathematical contributions to social and political science before the Second World War. Such treatments did exist; but they were scattered over three-quarters of a century in time and the entire Western world in space, frequently appearing in obscure journals or as minor parts of larger works and ranging in mathematical maturity from non-existent to occasional relative sophistication.

A similar situation confronts the Western bibliographer concerned with wei-ch'i. Brief mention of the game occurs in the memoirs and diaries of some pioneer European visitors to China—Matteo Ricci (Louis J. Gallagher [trans.], *China in the Sixteenth Century: The Journals of Matteo Ricci: 1582–1610*) and Alvarez Semedo (*Relatione della Grande Monarchia della Cina*, 1643)—and comes down to the present in some editions of Goren's *Hoyle* (for example,

New York: Greystone Press, Hawthorne Books, 1961).
Analyses range from the simple-minded exotica of "The
Orient's Ancient Game 'Go'" (an article in the *Japan Maga-
zine,* Tokyo, 1923, vol. 14, pp. 56–60) to highly technical
works by Japanese masters (see below). Places of publication extend from Shanghai via Tokyo and St. Paul, Minnesota to Philadelphia, Leipzig, and Dresden. Wei-ch'i literature is a collector's dream and a librarian's nightmare.

Attempts at classification may begin with the language
employed. In this regard, the literature displays surprising
homogeneity. Although it might be possible to unearth dis-
quisitions on the game in Portugese, Italian, or Dutch—to
say nothing of the possibilities in French or Russian (even
Latin has its representative: T. Hyde, *De Ludis Orientali-
bus. Libri Duo,* Oxford: E Theatro Sheldoniano, 1694)—all
important Western-language analyses of wei-ch'i, without
exception, are in English or German.

Turning first to the latter language, we may mention,
among others, O. Korschelt's "Das Go-spiel," a treatise
which appeared in several installments between 1880 and
1884 in the *Mitteilungen der deutschen Gesellschaft für
Natur- und Völkerkunde Ostasiens.* Korschelt's essay has
been translated by Samuel P. King and George G. Leckie
under the title *The Theory and Practice of Go* (Rutland,
Vermont and Tokyo: Charles E. Tuttle Co., 1966). There is
also a book by Bruno Rüger with the same title, *Das Go-
spiel, lehrbuch zur erlernung des ältesten brettspieles, mit
zahlreichen partien, aufgaben, eröffnungen und endspielen
japanischer meister, für anfänger und fortgeschrittene spieler*
(second edition, Leipzig: J. Klinkhardt, 1941; 158 pages
[first edition, Berlin, 1920]). Rüger reportedly also published
another book, *Handikap Go* (Dresden, 1929). Both of these
works are excellent serious and systematic treatments in the
German tradition. We should also mention a brief intro-

duction to go by one Leopold Pfaundler entitled *Das chinesisch-japanische Go-spiel. Eine systematische Darstellung und Anleitung zum Spielen desselben* (Leipzig: B. G. Teubner, 1908; 75 pages).

In English, brief but cogent descriptions of the Chinese game can be found in Samuel Couling's *Encyclopedia Sinica* (Shanghai: Kelly and Walsh, 1917), entry on wei-ch'i; and of the Japanese game go, or i-go, in Basil Hall Chamberlain, *Things Japanese* (London: Murray, 1902), entry on go. It is unfortunate for the present application of wei-ch'i that almost all English literature on the game deals with the Japanese rather than the Chinese version, though the differences are inessential for analogic purposes: the almost universal emphasis on go tends to obscure the origin of the Japanese game in Chinese wei-ch'i and the integral role of wei-ch'i in Chinese culture.

Explicitly concerned with the Chinese game are: Herbert A. Giles, "Wei-ch'i, or the Chinese Game of War" in *Temple Bar,* Volume xlix (1877), No. 194, 45–57, historically interesting for its emphasis on the difficulties encountered by the Westerner in the late nineteenth century seeking to learn how to play wei-ch'i and on the Chinese attitude toward the game; Z. Volpicelli, "Wei-ch'i" in the *Journal of the North China Branch of the Royal Asiatic Society,* Volume xxvi (1891–92), 80–107. Neither treatment gives significant material on strategy or tactics. We may also mention Edward Falkener's *Games Ancient and Oriental and How to Play Them* (New York: Dover, 1961; reprint of the 1892 edition of Longmans, Green and Company), which contains a fuzzy chapter on wei-ch'i, pages 239–50: the illustrative game included does, however, furnish an excellent example of how *not* to play. A later treatise, probably the most detailed of any on wei-ch'i in its Chinese incarnation, is by Count Daniele Pecorini and Tong Shu: *The Game of Wei-*

ch'i (London: Longmans, Green and Company, 1929; 128 pages).

By process of elimination, we have now arrived at what appears to be the hard core of Western knowledge about the "game of enclosing": English-language essays on go. On the most elementary level (discounting such oddities as Alice Howard Cady's *Go-bang; historical notes, with description of the original game, as played in China, Japan, etc., with a brief treatise on the English variety* [New York: American Sports Publishing Company, c. 1896; 25 pages]), we have sound basic treatments in Walter August De Havilland, *The ABC of Go, the National War Game of Japan* (Yokohama: Kelly and Walsh, 1910; 75 pages) and the more recent pamphlet of Lester and Elizabeth Morris, *The Game of Go* (American Go Association, 1951; 23 pages), one of the clearest expositions of the rules. On about the same level, but with flowery rhetoric on go and on the superiority of Japanese culture is Fukumensi Mihori, *The Japanese Game of "go,"* trans. by Zenchi Tamotsu Iwadō (Tokyo: Board of Tourist Industry, Japanese Government Railways, c. 1939; 76 pages; Tourist Library: 27), a brief summary designed for the casual reader.

Slightly more detailed and incorporating some basic strategico-tactical material is Gilbert W. Rosenthal's *A Go Primer* (Baltimore: mimeographed, 1943; 81 pages), which is devoted to go on the 13×13 board and describes rules as well as "minor" and general tactics. (The chapter on strategy is composed only of illustrative openings and games, with no orientation to general principles.) A similar, but considerably more detailed, work for the 19×19 version of the game is Arthur Smith's *The Game of Go, the National Game of Japan* (reprinted from the 1908 edition; Rutland, Vermont and Tokyo: Charles E. Tuttle Co., 1956; 220 pages): similar to Korschelt, it includes a sound description

195

of the rules, a chapter on the (principally Japanese) history of the game, and a few scattered remarks on tactics and operations; it contains many openings, corner positions, games, problems (with solutions), and a rather comprehensive Japanese-English glossary. Kaku Takagawa, a modern Japanese master of the highest caliber, has written *How to Play Go* (Tokyo: Japanese Go Association, 1956; 130 pages), a work for beginners but one with considerable theoretical orientation, which will repay close study. (See also Norio Kumabe, *Let's Play Go Today*, trans. by Masatsugu Tsuzawa and Donald C. Mann [Rutland, Vermont: Japan Publications Trading Company, 1964; 85 pages] and Shigemi Kishikawa, *Steppingstones to Go* [Rutland, Vermont and Tokyo: Charles E. Tuttle Co., 1965; 159 pages].)

Despite this catalogue of works on go, materials of genuine sophistication are scarce. Anyone can write a description of the rules and give illustrative examples with master comment taken from another source, but there are few Westerners competent to assess the strategy, or even the tactics, of the game or to discuss the works of Japanese masters which have been translated into English. One competent Western player has been the chess master Edward Lasker, also an accredited go player, whose *Go and Go-moku, the Oriental Board Games* (New York: Dover, second revised edition, 1960; 215 pages [first edition, 1934]), is probably the best book on the game in any Western language. Its value is in the differentiation of strategic and tactical material, the combination of theory with examples, and the remarkably high quality of those examples. As a source for investigation of the details of wei-ch'i, beyond the description in Chapter I of this work, this volume is highly recommended. Lasker has also written *Modern Chess Strategy, with an Appendix on Go* (second edition, revised, enlarged; New York: Mc-

Kay, 1950), essentially—in so far as it deals with wei-ch'i—a digest of his go book.

Two advanced works of Japanese masters, translated into the English language, should be noted. Kaku Takagawa's *The Vital Points of Go* (Tokyo: Japanese Go Association, 1958; 244 pages) is the most technical presentation of certain aspects of wei-ch'i strategy (no rule description is included) in a non-Asian language, containing sophisticated analysis of subtle problems, many of which would not even occur to an amateur, and interspersed with general observations of considerable profundity. Lasker's book *Go and Gomoku* bases its advanced strategy chapter on this volume of Takagawa. Of slightly different kind, but nevertheless of first-rate quality, is Kensaku Segoe, *Go Proverbs Illustrated*, trans. by John Bauer (Tokyo: Japanese Go Association, 1960, Go Library in English, Vol. I; 262 pages), a collection of analyses of forty-three maxims and principles, of which perhaps twenty are directly strategic in nature. This treatise, even more than Takagawa, is a mine of information for the Westerner interested in the underlying dynamics of higher wei-ch'i strategy.

Somewhat apart from these last-mentioned works, but still in its way relevant to advanced wei-ch'i theory, is John D. Goodell's *The World of Ki* (St. Paul, Minnesota: Riverside Research Press, 1957; 215 pages). This book is actually two volumes in one: a general theory of the structure and importance of games in human knowledge; and a treatise on go. (The "ki" of the title is the Japanese reading of "ch'i," as in "wei-ch'i.") An exhaustive account of the rules of the game is included, with a few supplementary observations on tactics and strategy which—though elementary in contrast to those in the Japanese works just cited—are occasionally provocative. Included is a stimulating chapter on pattern in go and its strategic significance. Goodell also mentions as forthcoming an essay by Karl Davis Robinson and John M. H. Olmsted on "The Structure of Go." This work was never published, but a précis appeared in the *Go Monthly Review*, 4.9 (September 1964), pages 87–103.

As for go/wei-ch'i periodical literature, lack of sustained popular interest in the game has prevented survival of several attempted Western journals, but we may mention in particular *The American Go Journal* published irregularly from 1949 by the American Go Association at Hackensack, New Jersey; *The Japanese Go Journal*, 1954–56; and the *Go Letter*, last published in New York by Takao Matsuda, 1962–64. A *Go Monthly Review* was founded in Tokyo in 1961 by the Japanese Go Association. The majority of contributions to these sundry periodicals are highly techno-tactical analyses of variations and opening patterns comparable to those found in Western chess works. However, occasionally essays of more general or strategic interest are included. In particular, we mention *The American Go Journal: An Anthology* (American Go Association, n.d.; 48 pages), a collection of articles which appeared in *The American Go Journal* over a period of years, as excellent supplementary reading to accompany a basic text such as Lasker. Much material on basic strategy and tactics, as well as on corner openings, general operations, handicap play, and master games, is included. Especially recommended for relevancy to "military wei-ch'i" is the section on nine-stone general openings written by a Japanese master and translated by L. S. Yang.

On the Korean game pa-tok (= go, wei-ch'i), we recommend pages 91–100 of Stewart Culin, *Korean Games, with Notes on the Corresponding Games of China and Japan* (Philadelphia: University of Pennsylvania Press, 1895), reprinted by the indefatigable Charles E. Tuttle firm as

Games of the Orient: Korea, China, Japan (1958; 177 pages). Both editions contain the interesting observation (p. 100 of each): "The game of Go is extremely popular in Japan at the present time, and is much played by military men, who regard it as an exercise in military tactics and instructive in the art of war."

Reversi, a game of the modern West with some resemblance to wei-ch'i, is treated in W. H. Peel, *Reversi and Gobang* (New York: F. A. Stokes and Company, 1890, 72 pp.), published under the pseudonym "Berkeley."

Finally, no bibliography of wei-ch'i, go, and war would be complete without mention of that tour de force *Japanese Chess (shō-ngi). The Science and Art of War or Struggle Philosophically Treated. Chinese Chess (Chong-kie) and I-go* by Cho Yo (Eurasiamerica/New York: The Press Club of Chicago, 1905; 242 pages). The objective of this magnum opus is best described by the author (p. 11):

> The writer is wholly convinced that if any one would a little study the easy movements of the pieces of this fascinating chess war, he will, without doubt, understand how the brain is easily improved and his nerves will be tempered and hardened; and the author fully hopes that his mental faculty, brightened, sharpened and advanced by maneuvers, tactics, diplomacy, strategy of wise men and generals on minimized battlefields on a small board upon a table— the maps of real warfares or struggles—would surely contribute one of the greatest shares for the *everlasting promotion* of the GREATEST REPUBLIC, THE UNITED STATES OF AMERICA, the FIRST in *peace* and FIRST in the hearts of all nations, and for its *supremacy to oversee* and *direct* the whole world for the sake of SUBLIME HUMANITY.

With this exposition of the principle of what he calls "chessologics," or "the Ultra-Philosophic Science," as a regulating principle of human struggle, Cho Yo proceeds to claim priority for Japanese chess (the Japanese analogue of Chinese hsiang-ch'i) in the following words (p. 10):

> The little people with a comparatively large quantity of gray-matter in their intellectual case have improved Chess according to their peculiar ingenuity of inventions, discoveries . . . and therapeutic advancement.

Japanese chess, he claims, is the "differential and integral calculus of chessology."

Of go, Cho Yo has less to say, but remarks rather cryptically (p. 214):

> The author forecasts in considering the differences between Chess and *Go,* or *Igo* that the latter would take far longer time than the former, if ever to be studied and played in other parts of the world, on account of lack, in the Western world of amusements, of affinity in regard to *Igo,* a kind of affinity existing in the two principal divisions or branches of Chessdom.

It is the purpose of this bibliographical note, and the hope of *The Protracted Game,* to minimize this predicted time-lag in Western understanding of wei-ch'i.

APPENDIX III

Artificial board. A military or political board whose boundaries are predominantly determined by legal or administrative considerations.

Board. In wei-ch'i, a grid upon which stones are played. By political analogy, the population of a geographic region. By military analogy, any geographic region (only occasionally two or more unconnected regions considered as a whole).

Capture. In wei-ch'i, removal from the board of certain stones of one side as a result of complete encirclement by forces of the other side. By political analogy, disaffection or other neutralization of the supporters of a given side or faction by non-violent means (for example, by propaganda). By military analogy, destruction, dispersal, or capture of a hostile military unit.

Collection. In wei-ch'i, any set of stones or groups of stones of one side which that side can connect at will; loosely, a set of stones or groups in a common pattern. By analogy, military or political forces of a side deployed in positions of close contact.

201

Corner opening. In wei-ch'i, a sequence of moves centering around attack or defense of a corner initially vacant or occupied by a single handicap stone.

Dead (group). In wei-ch'i, any group not yet captured but capturable at the will of the encircling player. By politico-military analogy, a permanently immobilized antagonistic group.

Distance from the edge of the board. In wei-ch'i, the number of intersections intervening between a given intersection and the edge. By political analogy, the socio-economic status of an individual or group; the more marginal the status, the nearer it is to the edge. By military analogy, the degree of military mobility permitted by the terrain of a given (small) geographic area.

Early middle game. In wei-ch'i, moves 50 ± 10 to 100 ± 10. Politico-military analogies dependent on a variety of variables.

Encirclement. In wei-ch'i, surrounding of a set of intersections so as to leave no unblocked exits on the periphery. By political analogy, political domination of an individual or set of individuals by control of the psychological stimuli to which they are exposed. By military analogy, surrounding of a given territorial area by military forces, possibly in conjunction with topographic factors.

End game. In wei-ch'i, approximately move 180 to termination of play (generally, about move 250). In politics or war, the concluding phases of a wei-ch'i-type conflict.

General opening. In wei-ch'i, an opening strategy or sequence covering the entire board; contrasted with the corner opening.

Group. In wei-ch'i, a set of two or more stones of one color arranged in a connected pattern (loosely extended to describe a single stone). No formal politico-military analogy, but to be understood as a particularly cohesive collection (see Collection).

Handicap. In wei-ch'i, black stones placed on the board in a conventional pattern before the game begins to *assist* a weak player in confronting a stronger. By political analogy, the political resources of a given side at the time when an opponent enters the theater of operations. By military analogy, the military power of such a side.

Note: whereas in Western usage a handicap customarily is a disadvantage to the individual possessing it, in wei-ch'i parlance a handicap gives positive payoff to the handicapped side.

Handicap player. In wei-ch'i, in politics or war, the side with a handicap.

Handicap points. In wei-ch'i, nine standard intersections on the grid-board, each indicated by a heavy dot. By political analogy, individuals politically active on behalf of a given side at the time when an opponent enters the theater of operations. By military analogy, areas militarily dominated by such a side.

Hsien-shou (Japanese sente). The wei-ch'i concept of initiative, or "having the move," which necessitates protective rather than independent play on the part of the opponent.

Intersection. In wei-ch'i, a point on the grid-board where a horizontal and a perpendicular line cross. On a political board, an individual or small group. On a military board, an indeterminate small geographic region.

Kill. To render an enemy force dead. See entry under "Dead (group)."

Linear group. In wei-ch'i, a group displaced so as to approximate a simple arc. By analogy, military forces positionally defending the entirety of a continuous sector: holding a line.

Middle game. In wei-ch'i, moves approximately 50 to approximately 180. Various politico-military analogies.

Natural board. A military or political board whose boundaries are natural physical obstacles, or a political board whose boundaries are socio-cultural-ethnic transition points.

No-handicap side. Side without a handicap (see Handicap).

Opening. In wei-ch'i, moves 1 to approximately 50. The opening phases of a wei-ch'i-type political or military conflict.

Side. In wei-ch'i, in politics or war, any strategically significant and integrated conflict force.

Sphere of influence, or influence. In wei-ch'i, any set of intersections under the (perhaps unconsolidated) hegemony of the stones of a given side. By political analogy, the supporters of a given political faction. By military analogy, any region at least loosely controlled by a side.

Stone. In wei-ch'i, a piece or marker; black or white. By political analogy, an active supporter of a given side, a cadre; also a small group of supporters or cadres. By military analogy, a soldier or more especially a military unit of reasonable size.

Territory. In wei-ch'i, intersections which will certainly be encircled by a given side at the end of the game. By political analogy, hard-core and organized supporters of a political faction, generally excepting party members (who might better be considered as stones). By military analogy, regions tightly controlled by the military forces of a side. *Potential territory:* intersections which will probably be encircled by a given side at the end of the game.

NOTES

1. Such phrases as "Western strategic tradition" and "Western warfare," used both in the text and in this footnote, are not, of course, intended to refer to any such homogeneous and crystallized body of doctrine as does the expression "the thought of Mao Tse-tung." French military principles have at times differed radically from those of the Germans, the system of Napoleon from that of Frederick, and the theories of Jomini from those of Clausewitz. Because of the partial lack of unity in Western strategy, all perceived differences between it and its Chinese counterpart must depend upon points of emphasis and orientation rather than upon absolute logical antitheses. In general, however, all Western military strategic doctrine, past and present, is based upon common historical experience and upon a common set of strategic concepts; and, further, historical Western military systems have greatly influenced one another and have tended to imitate each other's strong points. When the totality of Western strategic thought is set against that of China, fundamental common bonds outweigh differences of style and of interpretation.

2. This point is most generally recognized in connection with the differences between so-called "Eastern" and "Western" concepts of negotiation. See Henry A. Kissinger, *Nuclear Weapons and Foreign Policy* (New York: Harper, 1957), pp. 335–40.

3. Frank O. Hough (Major, USMCR), *The Island War* (Philadelphia: J. B. Lippincott, 1947), pp. 83–84.

4. *Army Digest,* 22.2 (February 1967), p. 41, quoting General William C. Westmoreland.

5. The assertion in the text does not claim that the Chinese Communist party has had actual control over strategy selection on the part of the Viet Minh, Pathet Lao, or various other insurgent groups. What is meant is that, questions of influence and imitation aside, a strong objective similarity is apparent between many motifs of the strategy of the Chinese Communists and that of the majority of Southeast Asian Communist insurgents.

6. On general simulation models (and bibliography on the subject) see Richard A. Brody, "Some Systemic Effects of the Spread of Nuclear Weapons Technology: a Study through Simulation of a Multi-Nuclear Future," *The Journal of Conflict Resolution*, 7.4 (December 1963). Mr. Brody defines (p. 671) *simulations* as "physical and/or biological representations of systems which attempt to replicate sociopolitical processes."

7. Pronounced "way-chee."

8. One of the outstanding players of the twentieth century is a Chinese, Wu Ch'ing-yuan (who has adopted the Japanese name Go Seigen). At least one Chinese player in Taiwan (Lin Hai-feng) is currently a high-ranking master.

On the historical role of wei-ch'i in China see Herbert A. Giles, "Wei-ch'i, or the Chinese Game of War," in *Temple Bar*, 49.194 (1877), pp. 45–57. Some students of Chinese history sugest that the theories of the ancient Chinese strategist Sun Tzu bear distinct similarity to wei-ch'i dicta, an assertion rendered the more plausible given widely accepted congruences between Maoist doctrine and that of the ancient thinker. Wei-ch'i is mentioned in a military context in the *T'ang T'ai-tsung Li Wei-kung wen-tui* [*Dialogues between the emperor T'ai-tsung of the T'ang and Duke Li of Wei* (*Li Ching*)], which is one of the *Ch'i Shu* [*The Seven Books*], a collection of pronouncements on military theory which includes the Sun Tzu text. Perhaps more to the point, several leading strategists in the famous historical novel *San-kuo-chih yen-i* (translated by C. H. Brewitt-Taylor as *Romance of the Three Kingdoms* [2 vols.; Rutland, Vermont: Charles E. Tuttle Co., 1959]), said to have influenced Mao Tse-tung, played wei-ch'i. Tso Tsung-t'ang, a famous general of the late Ch'ing dynasty, was reputed to play two games of wei-ch'i daily, even when on campaign.

9. Mao Tse-tung, *Selected Military Writings* (Peking: Foreign Languages Press, 1963), p. 174. Hereafter cited as SMW.

10. SMW, p. 221. In view of the frequently didactic character of Mao Tse-tung's writings, the close similarity between the two quoted passages is significant: textual examination of the author's work shows that he tended to repeat, with elaborations, those passages which he thought most important for the consumption of his intended audience. The passage here quoted was reprinted, with suitable modifications to account for re-identification of the enemy, in *People's China* (August 1, 1950).

11. SMW, p. 377. The official translation given here renders the last word "chessboard." The reference, however, is to ch'i generically (thus including both hsiang-ch'i [Chinese chess] and wei-ch'i), and hence "chessboard" should be taken to mean "board."

12. For the official version of the Chinese text of the directive see *Mao Tse-tung hsüan-chi* (Peking: Jen-min ch'u-pan-she), IV, 1961, p. 1369. The wei-ch'i idiom for one's forces being safe, or one's position secure, is *huo,* literally "to live."

13. Irma E. Webber, *It Looks Like This* (New York: William Scott, 1949).

CHAPTER 1

1. Arthur Smith, *The Game of Go* (Rutland, Vermont: Charles E. Tuttle Co., 1956), p. 24, referring to O. Korschelt's statement in *The Theory and Practice of Go,* trans. by Samuel P. King and George G. Leckie (Rutland, Vermont: Charles E. Tuttle Co., 1966), pp. 259–60. While the scientific validity of Korschelt's claim is dubious, increase in board size undoubtedly produces an exponential increase in strategic complications. Thus, for instance, wei-ch'i on the 8×8 board is simple and almost purely tactical—by extension, an interesting commentary on chess.

2. Although theoretically, if a sufficient number of captures were made in the course of a game, this number of stones could be exhausted, in principle the number of men possessed by a wei-ch'i player is infinite.

3. It is significant of the difficulty of wei-ch'i that an inferior novice has been known to inflict a crushing defeat on a beginner playing his first game even though the beginner had been granted an extraordinary 27-stone handicap.

4. See John D. Goodell, *The World of Ki* (St. Paul, Minnesota: Riverside Research Press, 1957), p. 49, from which the idea of collection is taken in modified form.

5. The logic of capture theory is that, given such a safe group as described in the text, even if both regions into which that group's encircled intersections are dividable were reduced to one intersection each, the group would still contain two discontinuous intersections and would be similar to that group in Diagram 5 C.

Perhaps the best modern description of these rules may be found in Edward Lasker, *Go and Go-moku* (New York: Dover, 1960), especially pp. 4–10 and pp. 18–20.

6. Game-theoretically speaking, a group is dead if and only if, for every strategy vector available to the player to whom the group belongs, there exists a strategy vector of his opponent, the joint outcome of which will result in the capture of the group. That a counterstrategy exists does not, of course, imply that it will be used or even seen by the opponent: many beginners, through ignorance, allow the dead groups of their opponents to escape, and often masters will permit survival of a minor dead group in order to make greater gains elsewhere on the board. In theory, of course, the counterstrategy is effectively computable.

7. This example has been taken from Lester and Elizabeth Morris, *The Game of Go* (n.p.: American Go Association, 1951), p. 23.

8. A slightly different scoring technique is described in various late nineteenth-century accounts of the Chinese game: see, for example, Z. Volpicelli, "Wei-ch'i," *Journal of the North China Branch of the Royal Asiatic Society*, 26 (1891–92), pp. 106–7. By this variant method, the score of a side is based on the number of intersections under its domination at the end of the game, whether they are empty points of territory or occupied by stones of the appropriate color. The divergence between this scoring technique and that described in the text is not, however, as great as might be supposed.

9. *Ibid.*, p. 95.

10. In this characteristic, of course, wei-ch'i is like chess or checkers. It is in great part the differences in board size between the Asian game and these Western games that account for the discrepancy in duration.

11. For a similar line of thought see Smith, *The Game of Go.*, p. xi:

> Go, on the other hand, is not merely a picture of a single battle like Chess, but of a whole campaign of a modern kind, in which the strategical movements of the masses in the end decide the victory. Battles occur in various parts of the board, and some- times several are going on at the same time. Strong positions are besieged and captured, and whole armies are cut off from their line of communications and are taken prisoners unless they can fortify themselves in impregnable positions, and a far-reaching strategy alone ensures the victory.

Compare with Korschelt, *The Theory and Practice of Go,* pp. 6–7.

12. The growing influence in current game-theoretic literature of the concept of the non-zero sum game is creating a beneficial counter-trend to this essentially Western concept of complete victory; we may cite in particular Thomas C. Schelling's *The Strategy of Conflict* (New York: Oxford University Press, 1963).

13. In more precise language, we are arguing that wei-ch'i strategy is not that of a zero-sum game in which one player's gain is the other's loss. Of course, this point can be overstressed: in wei-ch'i, as in all two-person parlor games, the aim is to defeat the opponent, and in this sense wei-ch'i is purely competitive. In regard to *operational* strategy, however, the notion of wei-ch'i as a non-zero sum game is fruitful and may be retained without fear of contradiction. It is pos- sible for both sides to gain territory—and hence utility increments— without fierce competition; and, conversely, fierce engagements may result in losses for both sides when stones played in the combat oc- cupy intersections of potential territory.

It is noteworthy that the wei-ch'i concept of utility maximization in the sense of territorial control taking precedence over annihilation of enemy forces is strikingly similar to the sentiment enunciated by T. E. Lawrence—an unusually wei-ch'i-style Western military thinker—in describing Arab guerrilla operations in the First World War: "The Turkish army was an accident, not a target." ("Guerrilla Warfare," *Encyclopedia Britannica,* 1957 ed. [Chicago: Encyclopedia Britannica, Inc.], Vol. 10, p. 950B.)

14. Diagram 7 is adapted from Diagram 2, Chapter 10, Kaku Takagawa, *How to Play Go* (Tokyo: Japanese Go Association, 1956), p. 92.

15. Amplifying what is in the text, it must be cautioned that play *near* the edges of the board is not to be taken as play *on* the edges: the former maneuver encircles potential territory; the latter, for obvious reasons, does not. For this reason, "play in the corners" or "along the sides" means play near to the edge but three or four lines from it.

16. This highly stylized position is taken from an article by Koshi Takashima on end game play in *The American Go Journal: An Anthology* (n.p.: American Go Association, n.d.), pp. 16 ff.

17. *Ibid.* p. 17, Figure 6.

18. Smith, *The Game of Go,* glossary entry under *"Sente"* (Japanese transliteration of *hsien-shou*); see also p. 62, upon which much of the discussion in the text is based.

19. See, for example, Lasker, *Go and Go-moku,* p. 62: "During the opening stage of the game Sente (=*hsien-shou*) expresses itself only through threats to wall off large territories."

20. It should be noted that this White capture—though offensive in character—may not necessarily preserve *hsien-shou*; no immediate threats are posed to which Black must reply. The present example is taken from Kensaku Segoe, *Go Proverbs Illustrated,* trans. by John Bauer ("Go Library in English," Vol. 1 [Tokyo: Japanese Go Association, 1960]), p. 213.

21. Example adapted from Smith, *The Game of Go,* p. 210, problem 4.1.

22. Kaku Takagawa, *The Vital Points of Go* (Tokyo: Japanese Go Association, 1958), p. 18, quoting Wu Ch'ing-yuan.

23. On overconcentration see Segoe, *Go Proverbs Illustrated,* pp. 115–19.

24. Lawrence, "Guerrilla Warfare," p. 950C.

25. This point of strategy should be contrasted with its counterpart in chess where deliberate sacrifice of a piece is regarded as a mark of consummate skill. In wei-ch'i, hardly a game passes without a similar outlay of force.

26. Example adapted from Takagawa, *The Vital Points of Go,* p. 118, Diagram 81.

27. See Goodell, *The World of Ki,* pp. 94–103 for a useful and non-

technical description of the "new school." Among the notable works of Wu Ch'ing-yuan, we may cite his *Go Seigen iki zenshū* [*Collected Games of Wu Ch'ing-yuan*] (Tokyo: Tokyo Bunge Shunshu Shinsha, 1949–51).

CHAPTER 2

1. For a potentially relevant discussion of the general theory of analogy by a logician, see Joseph M. Bochenski, *The Logic of Religion* (New York: New York University Press, 1965), pp. 156–62, in which analogy is conceived as a hexadic relationship and analyzed in terms of mathematical logic. See also chapter 8, by the same author, in Albert Menne (ed.), *Logico-Philosophical Studies* (Dordrecht: Reidel, 1962).

For a provocative book-length instance of informal analogy, in contradistinction to the highly formal theories just mentioned, see Bruce Mazlish, *The Railroad and the Space Program* (Cambridge, Massachusetts: Massachusetts Institute of Technology Press, 1965).

From another point of view, we may consider the wei-ch'i "analogy" to be an instance of homomorphic reduction of a socio-cultural structure. For this concept see Harrison C. White, "A View on Mathematical Sociology" (Cambridge, Massachusetts: unpublished, 1967).

2. For a detailed study of the historical problems involved here see Jerome Ch'en, "Defining Chinese Warlords and their Factions," *Bulletin of the School of Oriental and African Studies, University of London*, 31, Part 3 (1968), pp. 563–600.

3. In fact, four-player wei-ch'i has been played on occasion in Western countries.

4. In order to maximize the over-all plausibility and consistency of the wei-ch'i hypothesis, however, the use of analogic wei-ch'i is kept to a minimum in ensuing sections, and all examples are taken from the conventional game.

5. The dichotomy adopted in the text might be criticized on the ground that the non-military conflict systems of a revolution can be further subdivided into political, social, economic, etc. Further subdivision would, however, exponentially increase the complexity of the model and hence decrease its efficacy; for operational purposes the geographic/human-level antithesis is sufficient.

6. In the Chinese case, this lability of sides in the political situation was most pronounced in the years 1927–35. In that period, it is often difficult to identify the "Nationalists" with any one player, unless it be that faction personally loyal to Chiang Kai-shek.

7. A graphic if oversimplified description of the dynamics of Chinese military politics in the republican period has been given by the British military thinker Cyril Falls in *A Hundred Years of War* (London: Gerald Duckworth, 1953), p. 242. Reprinted by permission.

The subtleties of war lords' wars sometimes appeared comic to European eyes. With more reason the simplicities of warlike Europeans appeared puerile to the Chinese. A perspicacious European war minister or commander might see two moves ahead. A Chinese war lord, when he applied himself to the job, could double that. War lord X, facing an offensive by war lord Y, had large, well-armed forces and was confident of victory; but his lieutenants, who may be called X_1 and X_2, "thought of their own interests." That is to say, they decided either to stand out of the fight or merely go through the motions of fighting, so that one of them—after having eliminated the other—might seize the opportunity to replace X, or alternatively to take service with Y. X in his extremity called upon Z, a war lord of equal standing and a member of his confederacy. But Z did not respond. He was delighted to see his old ally discomfited. His own good army was strengthened by that of X and he decided to settle his account with Y. He had waited too long, however; Y had meanwhile undermined his authority with *his* sub-war lords and went on to win another victory.

8. For interesting insights concerning boundaries of boards see Carl von Clausewitz, *On War,* trans. by Colonel J. J. Graham (London: Routledge and Kegan Paul, 1956), II, p. 2.

9. For basic data on the geopolitical characteristics of China see Joseph Needham, *Science and Civilization in China* (Cambridge: Cambridge University Press), I, 1954, pp. 55–72. See also the chapter entitled "Geography and Military Strategy" in Hsieh Chiao-min, *China: Ageless Land and Countless People* (Princeton, New Jersey: Van Nostrand, 1967), pp. 45–61.

10. Various concepts of graph theory (that of a dominating set, the kernel of a graph, its degree of connectivity, etc.) are relevant here. For a sociological application of some of these ideas see James S. Coleman, *Introduction to Mathematical Sociology* (New York: Free Press of Glencoe, 1964), Chapter 14, "Measures of Structural Characteristics."

11. The classic Chinese Communist analysis of this topic, though somewhat dated in terms of later development, is Mao Tse-tung's 1926 essay "Analysis of the Classes in Chinese Society," *Selected Works of Mao Tse-tung* (Peking: Foreign Languages Press), I, 1964, pp. 13–19.

12. A theory of social structure bearing distinct relation to the analogy developed in the text is presented in Johan Galtung, "Foreign Policy Opinion as a Function of Social Position," *Journal of Peace Research,* 3–4 (1964), pp. 206–31. In the article, Galtung maps socio-economic status onto a two-dimensional spatial configuration similar to the wei-ch'i board, the socio-economic status of a given individual being inversely proportionate to his nearness to the center of the plane region.

From a more theoretical viewpoint, it is possible that a systematic foundation to this part of our formal analogy could be discovered in the topological perspectives of field-theoretically oriented social scientists. See, in particular, Kurt Lewin, *Principles of Topological Psychology* (New York: McGraw-Hill, 1936) and the works of various of his disciples.

13. Compare the qualitative functional analyses of Herbert Simon in *Models of Man* (New York: Wiley, 1957) which attempt to derive results on small group interaction processes without specifying the quantitative features of the functions involved.

14. In particular, we may note the importance of such completely or partially immobile units as local guerrilla infrastructures or guerrilla bands in supplying intelligence and routine security duties.

15. Lasker, *Go and Go-moku,* p. 108.

16. See the useful article by George A. Kelly, "Revolutionary Warfare and Psychological Action," in Franklin Mark Osanka (ed.), *Modern Guerrilla Warfare* (New York: Free Press of Glencoe, 1962), pp. 425–38.

17. On game-theoretic models of strategic information see the clas-

sic discussion in John von Neumann and Oskar Morgenstern, *Theory of Games and Economic Behavior* (Princeton: Princeton University Press, 1953), Chapter II.

18. Samuel B. Griffith, *Mao Tse-tung on Guerrilla Warfare* (New York: Frederick A. Praeger, 1961), p. 23. For a Chinese Communist statement of the importance of complete intelligence, with special reference to the socio-political dimension, see Gene Z. Hanrahan (ed.), *Chinese Communist Guerrilla Tactics* (n.p.: mimeographed, 1952), p. 91.

CHAPTER 3

1. *The American Go Journal: An Anthology*, p. 3; see also p. 9: "The basic principle of strategy [in wei-ch'i] is to play first in the corners . . . then to build territory along the sides; and finally extending into the center."

2. See, in particular, Benjamin I. Schwartz, *Chinese Communism and the Rise of Mao* (Cambridge, Massachusetts: Harvard University Press, 1952), Chapter 5, "An Appraisal of Key Trends." Schwartz notes that, even in 1927, Mao himself was not militarily oriented (p. 84).

3. A systematic treatment of intraparty factionalism is given in Schwartz, *Chinese Communism*. See also Maurice Meisner, *Li Ta-chao and the Origins of Chinese Marxism* (Cambridge, Massachusetts: Harvard University Press, 1967) for an appraisal of the intellectual history of the movement to 1927; and John E. Rue, *Mao Tse-tung in Opposition, 1927–35* (Stanford, California: Stanford University Press, 1966). Documentary treatment is given in Hsiao Tso-liang, *Power Relations within the Chinese Communist Movement, 1930–34* (Seattle: University of Washington Press, 1961).

Bibliography relevant to the entire Kiangsi period in all its historical and strategic aspects is contained in Hsüeh Chün-tu, *The Chinese Communist Movement, 1921–37* (Stanford, California: The Hoover Institution, 1960).

4. On the soviets, no comprehensive historical treatment in a Western language exists, but basic data are summarized in articles in Howard L. Boorman (ed.), *Biographical Dictionary of Republican China* (Vol. 1, New York: Columbia University Press, 1967). See

also later volumes, to be published. Considerable detail may also be found in Jerome Ch'en, *Mao and the Chinese Revolution* (London: Oxford University Press, 1965).

5. While systematic support for these assertions must await comprehensive study of the period, adequate general evidence for the present purpose may be found in James E. Sheridan, *Chinese Warlord: The Career of Feng Yü-hsiang* (Stanford: Stanford University Press, 1966), Chapter 1, "Emergence of the Warlords." For ex post facto Chinese Communist perception of the situation in the years around 1927 see *Selected Works of Mao Tse-tung,* "Report on an Investigation of the Peasant Movement in Hunan," I, pp. 23–56.

6. For a technical study see Takagawa, *The Vital Points of Go,* p. 68 ("On Choosing to Slide Under the Stone at the Four-Four Point"). Description of two through nine stone handicaps may be found in Lasker, *Go and Go-moku,* pp. 78–79.

7. A remark in *The American Go Journal: An Anthology,* p. 9, is pertinent. *"These fourth line plays are designed for center influence,* more than immediate territorial gain." (Italics added.)

8. Compare the concept of elite strategy in Harold Lasswell, "Agenda for the Study of Political Elites," in Dwaine Marvick (ed.), *Political Decision-makers* (New York: Free Press of Glencoe, 1961) For a socio-political analysis of one warlord's attempts to base his authority on more enduring popular ground see Donald G. Gillin, *Warlord: Yen Hsi-shan in Shansi Province* (Princeton: Princeton University Press, 1967).

9. Diagram 11 is contained in Kaku Takagawa, *How to Play Go,* p. 44, as Diagram 4. It must, of course, be stressed that this position is highly artificial and is employed only for illustrative purposes.

10. Diagram 12 is contained in Takagawa, *How to Play Go,* p. 90, as Diagram 1.

11. Thus John K. Fairbank, *The United States and China* (Cambridge, Massachusetts: Harvard University Press, 1958), p. 164: "Other warlord areas were *centered around key economic regions* such as the Canton delta, the Chengtu plain in Szechwan, or the lower Yangtze valley around Shanghai and Nanking," and p. 176: "Chiang Kai-shek with the support of the more conservative leaders of the Kuomintang . . . *aimed at the rich strategic center* of the lower Yangtze." (Italics in both quotations added.)

12. Sheridan, *Chinese Warlord,* p. 18:

The more intelligent and ambitious warlords attempted to train their men into reasonably efficient and disciplined organizations. Other warlords did little in this regard, and their forces, although sometimes huge in numbers, were weak and inefficient.

13. *Ibid.,* p. 22 on competition for Peking.

14. It is an interesting psychological point that frequently to a wei-ch'i novice a territory in the center will seem much larger than it actually is (refer again to Diagram 11). Pattern-recognition literature might significantly relate to applied wei-ch'i analysis.

15. See the work of the late Marxist economist Chi Ch'ao-ting, *Key Economic Areas in Chinese History* (London: G. Allen and Unwin, 1936); these districts are asserted by Chi to have been for centuries the centers of agriculture, industry, and commerce in China.

16. For instance, for a few weeks in 1927 the Communists had a soviet in eastern Kwangtung province.

17. For example, the Nationalist *pao-chia* (mutual responsibility and surveillance) system was really a method of wei-ch'i political territorization but was never extensively implemented on a national scale.

18. Many proletariat-oriented Communist party officials accepted the peasant but only in a secondary capacity; see, for example, Schwartz, *Chinese Communism,* p. 124.

19. Mao Tse-tung, *Selected Works,* I, p. 18.

20. *Ibid.,* "Analysis of the Classes in Chinese Society," pp. 13–19.

21. On Changsha see Schwartz, *Chinese Communism,* p. 144.

22. A suggestive fictionalized account of the strategic psychology of chess which may underlie revolution by city uprisings is John Brunner, *The Squares of the City* (New York: Ballantine, 1965).

23. See Stuart R. Schram, *The Political Thought of Mao Tse-tung* (New York: Frederick A. Praeger, 1963), pp. 181–82.

24. Lasker, *Go and Go-moku,* p. 63.

25. SMW, p. 72.

26. Example from Segoe, *Go Proverbs Illustrated,* pp. 236–37.

27. For analysis see Schwartz, *Chinese Communism,* p. 190. Compare David Galula, *Counterinsurgency Warfare: Theory and Practice* (New York: Frederick A. Praeger, 1964), p. 36.

28. The history of republican Chinese provincialism has yet to be written. See again, however, Map 2, which may give some idea of the close relation between spheres of influence and provincial boundaries.

29. A basic Chinese Communist doctrinal pronouncement concerning the encirclement campaigns is Mao Tse-tung's December 1936 "Strategy in China's Revolutionary War," SMW, pp. 75–145, especially Chapter 5, pp. 101–45. Some editions of this essay contain maps of the Kiangsi campaigns (for example, *Chung-kuo ko-ming chan-cheng-ti chan-lüeh wen-t'i* [Hsin-min-chu ch'u-pan-she, 1949]). More general historical background is furnished in Ch'en, "Defining Chinese Warlords and Their Factions." An article in large part tacitly based upon the wei-ch'i perspectives here detailed is Howard L. and Scott A. Boorman, "Chinese Communist Insurgent Warfare, 1935–49," *Political Science Quarterly*, 81.2 (June 1966), pp. 171–95, especially pp. 178–84 on defensive strategy.

30. SMW, p. 236.

31. *Ibid.*, p. 110 on the former view, admittedly from a biased standpoint.

32. Takagawa, in *The Vital Points of Go*, pp. 98–100 deals with what he calls "light" and "heavy" plays, the distinction being somewhat comparable to that between a thrust with a rapier and a blow with a club (see also *The American Go Journal: An Anthology*, p. 33, where the adverb "lightly" appears in a translation from the Japanese by L. S. Yang). Compare Lasker, *Go and Go-moku*, p. 108 in a passage already quoted on mobility of stones. Later, he relates this notion to the topic of economy of influence.

33. Segoe, *Go Proverbs Illustrated*, p. 157 (in a chapter entitled "Don't play in direct contact with the opponent's stone caught in your squeeze-play").

34. See Général d'Armée André Beaufre, *An Introduction to Strategy*, trans. by Major General R. H. Barry (London: Faber and Faber, 1965).

35. Smith, *The Game of Go*, pp. 60, 62.

36. *The American Go Journal: An Anthology*, p. 33.

37. Segoe, *Go Proverbs Illustrated*, p. 158. To prevent confusion it is, however, desirable to add one point. Maoist strategic retreat, even as its wei-ch'i counterpart, is only a conditional matter, dependent upon a significantly discrepant counterinsurgent/insurgent strength differential. Under conditions in which discrepancy is absent, neither

Maoist theory nor wei-ch'i practice involves the withdrawal motif. Compare our treatment of wei-ch'i strategy on pp. 28–29; SMW, p. 115; and Boorman and Boorman, "Chinese Communist Insurgent Warfare," p. 180, fn. 18.

38. The first quotation is from Mao Tse-tung, *Strategic Problems of China's Revolutionary War* (n.p.: Tung-pei hsin-hua shu-tien, 1949), p. 70; the second is from SMW, p. 131.

39. SMW, p. 80.

CHAPTER 4

1. Certainly erroneous, however, is Anthony Garavente's contention in *The China Quarterly*, 22 (April–June, 1965), p. 93, that the Communist defeat in the fifth encirclement campaign against Kiangsi bases was due to an inherent inconsistency between territorial control and mobile warfare: the existence of wei-ch'i as a coherent conflict system embodying both motifs would seem adequate refutation.

2. Segoe, *Go Proverbs Illustrated*, pp. 207–11.

3. English language surveys relevant to general matters of strategy in the Sino-Japanese war of 1937–45 are Evans F. Carlson, *The Chinese Army* (New York: Institute of Pacific Relations, 1940); Tang Tsou, *America's Failure in China, 1941–50* (Chicago: University of Chicago Press, 1963); and Harold S. Quigley, *Far Eastern War, 1937–41* (Boston: World Peace Foundation, 1942). A history from the Japanese standpoint is Hata Ikuhiko, *Nit-chū sensōshi* [*The Sino-Japanese War*] (Tokyo: Kawade Shobō Shinsha, 1961).

4. Sources on Chinese Communist expansion, 1937–45, include Chalmers Johnson, *Peasant Nationalism and Communist Power* (Stanford, California: Stanford University Press, 1962); Lionel Max Chassin, *L'Ascension de Mao Tse-tung, 1921–45* (Paris: Payot, 1953); and, in Chinese, *K'ang-Jih chan-cheng shih-ch'i-ti Chung-kuo jen-min chieh-fang-chün* [*The Chinese People's Liberation Army in the Period of the War of Resistance against Japan*] (Peking: Jen-min ch'u-pan she, 1953).

5. George E. Taylor, *The Struggle for North China* (New York: Institute of Pacific Relations, 1940), pp. 76, 78.

6. In the period under discussion, air power was a negligible factor: contemporary Communist texts barely mention it. The concept of military control here set forth would, therefore, have to be revised

for application to analysis of revolutionary situations in la~

7. Taylor, *Struggle for North China*, p. 49.

8. *Ibid.*, p. 55.

9. Possibly German influences on the Japanese may be in part ~ countable for anti-wei-ch'i patterns of Japanese strategy. But, at a deeper level, the adaptation of wei-ch'i to Maoist doctrine in the present volume constitutes only one possible interpretation of the abstract structure of the game. The Japanese military mind could conceivably have discovered resemblances to wei-ch'i on another analogic level. (For a remark on Japanese strategy and wei-ch'i see Smith, *The Game of Go*, p. 16.)

10. I. A. Horowitz, *How to Win in the Middle Game of Chess* (New York: McKay, 1955), p. 121.

11. See Introduction, pp. 6–7.

12. SMW, pp. 260–61.

13. This distinction does not occur in the literature and is derived from wei-ch'i.

14. See details contained in Lo Jui-ch'ing, "Political Work in Military Units," in Hanrahan (ed.), *Chinese Communist Guerrilla Tactics*, pp. 125 ff.

15. For elementary information on the highly developed wei-ch'i theory of extensions into new territories see *The American Go Journal: An Anthology*, pp. 10–11.

16. Johnson, *Peasant Nationalism*, p. 90.

17. SMW, p. 229.

18. *Ibid.*

19. Noteworthy in this respect is the slogan *"ch'üan-kuo i-pan ch'i"* emphasized by the Chinese Communists in the 1960's in connection with economic strategy. Literally, this expression means "the entire nation is a ch'i board." It is possible that the reference here is to wei-ch'i, not to hsiang-ch'i (the Chinese counterpart of Western chess).

20. Johnson, *Peasant Nationalism*, pp. 118–19.

21. See Mao Tse-tung, *Selected Works*, II, pp. 389–93: "Unite all anti-Japanese forces and combat the anti-Communist die-hards." There was, of course, harassment: see Johnson, *Peasant Nationalism*, p. 90.

22. See Chapter 1, fn. 8, on the variant scoring procedure. For more detail on Communist tactics, see Johnson, *Peasant Nationalism*, pp. 84 ff. and pp. 149–55.

23. See Johnson, *Peasant Nationalism and Communist Power* for a book-length analysis; a briefer study is the same author's *Revolution and the Social System* (Stanford, California: The Hoover Institution, 1964), especially p. 61.

On the tactics of the united front, one interesting model is developed in S.M. Chiu, *Chinese Communist Revolutionary Strategy, 1945–49* (Research Monograph No. 13, Center of International Studies, Princeton University, 1961), p. 21. The general idea underlying the symbolic equations of that author is one common in wei-ch'i strategy, though seldom explicitly articulated as a principle: namely, sequential offensive, in which encirclement and annihilation of one group is used to obtain a favorable position for the encirclement of a second group, and so on.

24. On the frequent fate of edge groups contained away from the center see, for example, *The American Go Journal: An Anthology*, p. 12; see also Lasker, *Go and Go-moku*, pp. 104–5.

25. See Chapter I, page 37 and fn. 27.

26. Boorman and Boorman "Chinese Communist Insurgent Warfare," p. 186; on the militia, see also Ho Kan-chih, *A History of the Modern Chinese Revolution* (Peking: Foreign Languages Press, 1959), pp. 396–401.

27. Compare Hanrahan (ed.), *Chinese Communist Guerrilla Tactics*, p. 65: "Guerrillas are in a position to completely paralyze the movements of the enemy, preventing him from either advancing or retreating."

28. For more detailed typology, see SMW, pp. 168–70.

29. See Hanrahan (ed.), *Chinese Communist Guerrilla Tactics*, which includes, in translation, several detailed essays relating to these three actions. In particular, see "A Textbook on Guerrilla Warfare" (pp. 75–93) and "Tactical Problems of Guerrilla Warfare" (pp. 94–112), the latter edited by Kuo Hua-jo, noted Chinese Communist military thinker and commentator on Sun Tzu.

30. Of course, not all physical encirclement was effected by the actual presence of Chinese units: difficult terrain—that is, the edge of the board—was also used extensively to realize four-sided isolation of

the enemy. Cf. Hanrahan (ed.), *Chinese Communist Guerrilla Tactics*, p. 86.

31. See Kuo Hua-jo, pp. 94–112, in *Chinese Communist Guerrilla Tactics*.

32. Opinion differs as to what constitutes the opening, the middle, and the end game in wei-ch'i. Smith, *The Game of Go*, p. 186, assigns moves 1–20 to the opening; 20–170 to the middle game; and 170–250 to the end game. However, several "openings" which he recounts in Chapter 6 are about 50 moves in length. Adoption of this last figure would make the middle game 120–130 plays in duration.

33. SMW, p. 222.

34. Diagram 16 is the same as Lasker, *Go and Go-moku*, p. 87, Diagram 24.

35. SMW, pp. 220–21 (already quoted in part in the Introduction). For similar emphasis upon the revolutionary war "mosaic" to which we have had occasion to compare a wei-ch'i game (Chapter I, p. 23), see Galula, *Counterinsurgency Warfare*.

36. Segoe, *Go Proverbs Illustrated*, p. 210, Diagram 4.

37. SMW, p. 220.

38. SMW, pp. 219–220.

39. It has been said that one difference between Russian and Chinese psychology is mirrored in the literatures of those nations: both handle themes of great magnitude and emphasize extended spaces; but Russian literature is set against vast empty spaces, whereas the Chinese counterpart has a background of swarming humanity. This is precisely the distinction which must be made in classifying types of guerrilla warfare.

40. SMW, pp. 167–68. The theme is also treated in Hanrahan (ed.), *Chinese Communist Guerrilla Tactics*, pp. 70–74.

41. This phenomenon is not uncommon. Sometimes a player will deliberately let one group escape in order to gain greater advantage elsewhere on the board; at other times, such relinquishment is defensively necessary to prevent even greater loss.

42. Brig. Gen. J. D. Hittle, U.S.M.C., Ret. (ed.), *Jomini and His Summary of the Art of War* (Harrisburg, Pennsylvania: Military Service Publishing Company, 1958), p. 76.

43. An alternate theoretical construct could identify the Japanese as the handicap player, the handicap consisting of Japanese and pro-

Japanese forces on the China board after the initial blitzkrieg. Chinese forces at that time, being weak or disorganized, could then be discounted, especially on the board of the occupied areas which we are considering most carefully, and the situation of Mao's model would be nearly similar to that in an actual handicap wei-ch'i game where the inferior player has the handicap.

44. This is probably the most serious error of the beginner; even a nine-stone handicap is insufficient for the purpose.

45. See the detailed description in *Kang-Jih chan-cheng shih-ch'i-ti Chung-kuo jen-min chieh-fang-chün,* pp. 9 ff.

46. Perhaps wei-ch'i strategy is best described by a series of topological axioms about the structure and composition of the playing field and the interrelation of the forces on it.

47. SMW, p. 254.

48. In one actual game between a Western player and a Chinese master of the lowest grade, the Westerner was given a four-stone handicap but finished the game with only one live group and a *negative* score of nearly 100 points. In this game, as in Mao's protracted war, battles of annihilation lasted throughout the end game: the final play killed the Western player's last group but one. Another even more extreme example is the following: a Western player of very modest knowledge played a novice in the latter's first (and presumably last) game. The amateur succeeded in wiping out the beginner's forces to the last man—or, rather, stone.

CHAPTER 5

1. Actually, all hope of peace negotiations was not relinquished by the Americans until early 1947; but, after the Japanese capitulation, fighting between the two factions had been developing on an ever-increasing scale.

2. As brief bibliography we may list, on the Chinese Communist side, in addition to the work of Ho Kan-chih already cited, Liao Kai-lung, *From Yenan to Peking* (Peking: Foreign Languages Press, 1954), a brief survey of the 1945–49 war; and, in Chinese, *Ti-san-tz'u kuo-nei ko-ming chan-cheng kai-k'uang* (Peking: People's Publishing House, 1954), which contains maps, chronologies, and statistical tables. Western analyses which must be taken into account, although of varying quality, are F. F. Liu, *A Military History of Modern China*

(Princeton, New Jersey: Princeton University Press, 1956), which is meager on battle detail; U.S. Department of State, *United States Relations with China* (Washington, D.C.: Government Printing Office, 1949), Chapter 7, "The Military Picture, 1945–49," which is oriented toward politico-economic background with, however, some relevant data; O. Edmund Clubb, *Twentieth Century China* (New York: Columbia University Press, 1964), a good historical description containing some campaign detail on the civil war; and Lionel Max Chassin, *The Communist Conquest of China: a History of the Civil War, 1945–49*, trans. by Timothy Osato and Louis Gelas, (Cambridge, Massachusetts: Harvard University Press, 1965), occasionally inaccurate but with maps and military orientation. Two particular campaigns, the Manchurian and the Huai-Hai, are detailed, respectively, in O. Edmund Clubb, "Manchuria in the Balance, 1945–1946," *Pacific Historical Review*, XXVI (1957), pp. 377–89, and the same author's "Chiang Kai-shek's Waterloo: the Battle of the Hwai-Hai," *Pacific Historical Review*, XXV (1956), pp. 389–99. Mao Tse-tung's *Selected Military Works* has useful footnotes on campaign operations but is without maps. Finally, a theoretical survey of the Chinese Communist offensive after 1947 is provided in Boorman and Boorman, "Chinese Communist Insurgent Warfare," pp. 184–88.

3. American planes airlifted elite Nationalist troops from west China to key points in the north and northeast: Nanking, Peking, etc. This operation constituted play of stones in literal wei-ch'i fashion.

4. Several large cities in Manchuria were under Communist control for a short period in 1945–46.

5. Relative to the problem of decomposition of boards, see the general analysis of subsystem decomposition in Franklin M. Fisher and Albert Ando, "Two Theorems on *Ceteris Paribus* in the Analysis of Dynamic Systems," *The American Political Science Review*, 56.1, (March 1962), pp. 108–13.

6. Robert B. Rigg, *Red China's Fighting Hordes* (Harrisburg, Pennsylvania: Military Service Publishing Company, 1951), p. 204, quoting a tactical manual by Lin Piao.

7. The upper left corner adjoins the Peking area; we are looking down toward the north China plain (off board to upper left) from about the Vladivostok district.

8. Takagawa, *The Vital Points of Go,* p. 2. Just as in the initial phases of Manchurian operations, only a few stones have been played; but those few will help to determine the future course of the conflict.

9. See Segoe, *Go Proverbs Illustrated,* pp. 188 ff.

10. *Ibid.,* pp. 223 ff.

11. See Smith, *The Game of Go,* p. 215 (problems), p. 216 (diagram), p. 220 (solutions). This complexity of the disconnecting operation contrasts with the simplicity of the patterns generally presented in Western military textbooks.

12. The problem of psychological encirclement and, in general, of operations on the human level board during the 1945–49 period presents a potential extension of the wei-ch'i analogy.

13. This same disproportionateness is a general phenomenon in wei-ch'i; compare with the example which follows in the text.

14. This example is taken from Lasker, *Go and Go-moku,* pp. 130–46, where the game in which these positions are contained is discussed. See Lasker's analysis of proper disconnection strategy, *Go and Go-moku,* p. 130. Diagrams 19–21 are based upon Lasker's diagrams 42–44. One important modification, however, has occurred: instead of being victorious as in our example, White actually suffered a defeat in the last few moves of disconnecting operations because of an elementary error which allowed Black to break out. To make the desired point in the text, White has been made to play the correct variation.

15. Refer to Needham, *Science and Civilization in China,* I, p. 62, where what we have called "north China" is divided into four distinct geographic regions: the Shantung mountains, the north China plain, the mountainous plateau of Shansi, and the Shensi basin. See also the geotectonic map, p. 65, and on economic geography, pp. 67–72.

16. Refer to pp. 93–94.

17. Wei-ch'i territory is, in a sense, a co-operative venture. Essentially what is said in the text is only another formulation of the principle of co-ordinated action set forth in Chapter I (pp. 33–34).

18. On pillbox psychology and its consequences see Rigg, *Red China's Fighting Hordes,* p. 256.

19. In master play, three successive wasted moves would probably lose the game. A more sophisticated discussion of waste and inefficiency in wei-ch'i is Takagawa, *Vital Points of Go,* pp. 74 ff., "On Scale in Planning."

20. An authority on counterinsurgency warfare once remarked that one of the greatest handicaps under which a counterinsurgent facing a (Maoist-type) revolution labors is the ingrained notion that advance —any advance—is a positive good. While perhaps applicable in a situation such as the Western front in the First World War, he continued, in a counterinsurgency situation the notion has no validity whatsoever.

21. This pattern of campaign is oversimplified but not injuriously so. For the entire story, see Clubb, *Twentieth Century China,* Chapter 8, "Kuomintang-Communist Struggle: Final Stage." See also Chassin, *The Communist Conquest of China,* pp. 121–26.

22. Also called the battle of Hsuchow (Suchow). The present analysis relies on O. Edmund Clubb, "Chiang Kai-shek's Waterloo: the Battle of the Hwai-Hai."

23. *Ibid.,* pp. 390–91.

24. *Ibid.,* p. 392. There was a personal quarrel between their commanders and those of the Seventh Army Group. One improvement in the sophistication of the wei-ch'i analogy would be the effective incorporation of n players. However, in practice, the two-player approximation generally suffices.

25. *Ibid.,* p. 393.

26. *Ibid.,* pp. 394–98.

27. Galula, *Counterinsurgency Warfare,* p. 134.

28. Of course, the construction of such nets of stones is desirable only when positively necessary; otherwise, negative payoff will result.

29. It has even been somewhat rashly claimed that, after 1945, the Chinese Communists did not need to employ any over-all strategic system but relied merely on effective tactics and logistics (for example, in Rigg, *Red China's Fighting Hordes,* p. 260). From the point of view of the wei-ch'i analogy, no assertion could be farther from the truth, although *to a beginner* the operations of the middle and end game may, in fact, *appear* to be nothing more than tactical maneuverings. It is this failure to understand the systemic structure of Chinese Communist insurgent warfare from beginning to end of the revolution that is the principal target of the wei-ch'i model.

30. Given a significant strength differential, we may almost categorically assert that the end game will be over when the final major battle of encirclement and annihilation is completed and that, throughout

most of the latter part of the game, large-scale annihilation will be the sole target of the superior player's strategic direction.

31. Rigg, *Red China's Fighting Hordes*, p. 216. The explanation for such attacks given by Rigg is logistical: rice is the objective. Perhaps this hypothesis is more suggestive of the logistically-oriented state of American military thought than illuminating of the Chinese Communist psyche.

32. A passage in Galula, *Counterinsurgency Warfare*, p. 86, is worth quoting in full:

> What could happen in default of control? The general counterinsurgency effort would produce an *accidental* mosaic, a patchwork of pieces with one well pacified, next to it another one not so pacified or perhaps even under the effective insurgent's control: an ideal situation for the insurgent, who will be able to maneuver at will among the pieces, concentrating on some, temporarily vanishing from others. The *intentional* mosaic created by necessity when the counterinsurgent concentrates his efforts in a selected area is in itself a great enough source of difficulties without adding to it in the selected area.

The wei-ch'i overtones of this paragraph are evident; compare chapter I, p. 23.

33. SMW, pp. 347–48.

34. Goodell, *The World of Ki*, p. 30.

35. Statistical study of the ratio of the magnitude of the encircling chain plus supporting forces to captured group would be interesting as a dimension of pure wei-ch'i with analogic implications. A guess might estimate the ratio average to be 3:1.

36. With the intensive development of quickly deployable counterinsurgent firepower, especially in the air, this principle is becoming more and more relevant in revolutionary warfare.

37. See Simon, *Models of Man*, p. 221.

CHAPTER 6

1. Throughout the following enumeration it will be understood that the referent of the term "insurgency" is what Galula, *Counterinsurgency Warfare*, p. 63, has defined as the "hot revolutionary war," that

is, the phase of insurgency in which the activity of the insurgent side becomes "openly illegal and violent." This is not to say, of course, that the wei-ch'i model does not have applicability to the cold—that is, essentially non-violent—revolution.

2. Edward L. Katzenbach and Gene Z. Hanrahan, "The Revolutionary Strategy of Mao Tse-tung," *Political Science Quarterly,* 70.3 (September 1955), p. 326, have defined space in military terms as "square mileage plus obstacles minus a workable communications network." It is in this sense—in the sense of space made relative to strategic mobility—that the geographic theater of revolutionary operations should be extensive in size. Thus Vietnam, although a small country in square mileage, is relatively large considering the lack of workable communications and the predominance of jungle terrain.

3. As pointed out on page 47, there is no formal real-life analogue to wei-ch'i territory. We, therefore, use the term "influence" as a realistic substitute.

4. This statement, and several which follow it, are normative statements, based upon experience with what generally happens in Maoist insurgencies, not upon what necessarily happens: *generally* an insurgency does not develop if the handicap is too great to start with; *generally* a jigsaw pattern, etc., manifests itself; and so on. The wei-ch'i features to which these normative descriptions are compared are similarly normative: *generally* a handicap is nine stones or fewer; *generally* we have a fluid pattern of dispersion, etc. This normativity should be kept in mind for investigation of possible "abnormal" conditions and their wei-ch'i parallels.

5. Boorman and Boorman, "Chinese Communist Insurgent Warfare," p. 182:

A second factor . . . was the concept of initiative. To the Western strategist, initiative is often a kinetic force directly based on offensive action. To the Chinese Communists, initiative was rather a potential force: it was freedom of action, the ability of the army to go where its commander wished it to go.

Compare with the discussion of *hsien-shou* in Chapter I, pp. 31–33.

6. On sacrifice, see Goodell, *The World of Ki,* p. 58, on the tactical use of suicide. In many patterns, capture cannot be realized without sacrificial loss.

7. Those virtues will dominate any list of the principles of war.

8. For a discussion of this last strategy, see Brigadier C. A. Dixon and O. Heilbrunn, *Communist Guerrilla Warfare* (New York: Frederick A. Praeger, 1955).

9. On iconic structure and military analysis, see Henry E. Eccles, Rear Admiral, U.S.N., Ret., *Military Concepts and Philosophy* (New Brunswick, New Jersey: Rutgers University Press, 1965), p. 284:

> The skillful use of a blackboard during a discussion provides a visualization of the problem as a whole, presenting the major factors of plans and ideas *simultaneously,* as on a blueprint. Thus it is easier to attain perspective and to distinguish the important from the trivial. In a purely verbal presentation, ideas are heard or read *sequentially;* and *since human memory is always faulty,* the comprehensive appreciation in one's mind becomes difficult when a sequential presentation is purely verbal, with no concurrent review of a picture of the problem as a whole.

Again, p. 113:

> In some instances the technique of using a game theory matrix as a visual aid to the commander in reaching a decision is worthwhile.

A similar observation would hold for the wei-ch'i model, even though, in it, the matrix idea is put to a somewhat different use.

To the author's knowledge, there are in the study of war, politics, and revolution few instances of use of concepts similar to the wei-ch'i model.

The September-October 1963 joint edition of the *Journal of Conflict Revolution* (7.3) and the *Journal of Arms Control* (1.4) contains (pp. 235–45 CR: pp. 329–339 AC) an article by Joan V. Bondurant, entitled "Paraguerrilla Strategy: a New Concept in Arms Control." This paper involves discussion of several analogies to revolution and the revolutionary process: one compares revolution to chemical catalysis; another, to certain processes in psychopathology; a third, to immunological physiology. The inadequacy of the three analogies when compared to wei-ch'i lies, of course, in that they each compare insurgency to a semi-mechanical process, whereas reality demands continuous choice and decision for all participants in revolution.

Survey, No. 46 (January 1963), an issue devoted to Soviet culture, includes (112–24) an article "Chess and Politics" by D. J. Richards; a subsequent book by the same author is entitled *Soviet Chess* (Oxford: Clarendon Press, 1965).

10. For a related treatment, see Howard L. and Scott A. Boorman, "Strategy and National Psychology in China," *The Annals of the American Academy of Political and Social Science*, No. 370 (March 1967), pp. 143–155.

11. In particular, cases of application, transferral, or influence have occurred at various times in Indochina, the Philippines, Malaya, Cuba, Algeria, and Angola, among others.

12. It might be interesting to investigate the relation of wei-ch'i/ Maoist territoriality to the concept of similar designation employed in bio-ecology and related fields.

13. It would be relevant to attempt to determine to what extent Sino-Soviet differences in the 1960's were the product of fundamental divergences in the strategic concepts of the Chinese decision-making elite and of the Russian, the former having a wei-ch'i orientation, the latter based on a non- or anti-wei-ch'i premise. Chess, it should be remembered, is in many ways very anti-wei-ch'i in its strategic structure.

14. William Shakespeare, *Coriolanus*, I, vii. For background material on the territorial concept of Maoist revolution see Robert W. McColl, "A Political Geography of Revolution: China, Vietnam, and Thailand," *The Journal of Conflict Resolution*, 11.2 (June 1967), pp. 153–67.

15. Samuel B. Griffith (trans.), *The Art of War* (Oxford: Clarendon Press, 1963), p. 91; B. H. Liddell Hart, *Strategy* (New York: Frederick A. Praeger, 1954), p. 347.

16. Compare with the section "The Concept of Confrontation" in Takagawa, *The Vital Points of Go,* pp. 16ff.

17. Griffith, *The Art of War,* p. 98.

18. Beaufre, *Introduction to Strategy,* p. 124.

19. For an interesting parallel between wei-ch'i and Communist strategy, see "Squeeze Play in Thailand?" in *The Reporter* (August 11, 1966) pp. 16–18, in which co-ordinated Communist pressures from the northeast and along the Malay-Thai border are discussed. The title is noteworthy: the "squeeze play" is a wei-ch'i motif (cf. Takagawa, *The Vital Points of Go,* pp. 36ff).

20. Mao Tse-tung, *On the Protracted War* (Peking: Foreign Languages Press, 1960), p. 60.

21. See Bernard B. Fall, *Street Without Joy* (third revised edition; Harrisburg, Pennsylvania: The Stackpole Company, 1963).

22. Goodell, *The World of Ki*, p. 29.

23. See Robert B. Rigg, "Red Parallel: the Tactics of Ho and Mao," in Osanka (ed.), *Modern Guerrilla Warfare*, p. 273, and Boorman and Boorman, "Chinese Communist Insurgent Warfare, 1935–49," p. 187.

24. Griffith, *The Art of War*, pp. 109–10: "Do not thwart an enemy returning homewards. To a surrounded enemy you must leave a way of escape. Do not press an enemy at bay." A similar thought is to be found in Vegetius: "The flight of an enemy should not be prevented, but facilitated." See Major Thomas R. Phillips, U.S. Army, *Roots of Strategy* (Harrisburg, Pennsylvania: Military Service Publishing Company, 1940), p. 164.

25. For a sophisticated analysis of Lin Piao's important statement in *The People's Daily* of September 3, 1965 entitled "Long Live the Victory of People's War," which has considerable bearing on the concept of ultimate complete victory discussed in the text, see D. P. Mozingo and T. W. Robinson, "Lin Piao on 'People's War': China Takes a Second Look at Vietnam," RAND Memorandum RM-4814-PR (November 1965).

As a cautionary antidote, see also George H. Quester, "On the Identification of Real and Pretended Communist Military Doctrine," *The Journal of Conflict Resolution*, 10.2 (June 1966), pp. 172–79.

26. Of course, as Fall points out in *Street Without Joy*, p. 308, no showdown was intended for 1953–54; but Dienbienphu ultimately developed into one.

27. We are referring in particular to the well-known human-wave assault patterns, used both by the Chinese Communists and by the Viet Minh at Dienbienphu.

28. Excellent statistical discussion of the outcome of Dienbienphu is to be found in appendices to Bernard B. Fall, *Hell in a Very Small Place* (Philadelphia: J. B. Lippincott, 1967). According to his figures, total French casualties were about 20,000. Of these only 2,204 represent men killed on the ground prior to collapse of the defense. A third of the losses—6,500 men—were prisoners taken *after* the position had been overrun, *hence presumably at no cost to the enemy.*

Viet Minh losses are reconstructed at 7,900 killed; 15,000, wounded. Assuming that the main position of a second Dienbienphu were not overrun, we may assume that the wounded statistics have very different significance for a modern army with modern medical facilities on the one hand and for a semi-guerrilla force on the other. In the second Vietnamese war statistics consistently show that a far higher proportion of American wounded recover combat readiness than do North Vietnamese and National Liberation Front casualties. Thus the kill ratio is further turned in favor of the defender in a Dienbienphu-type situation.

29. See Fall's discussion in *Hell in a Very Small Place.*

30. By way of caveat, it should be pointed out that the inflexibility of Maoist principles here postulated should not be confounded with the operational flexibility which is involved in the idea of strategic retreat. Paradoxically, the offense may be far less flexible than the defense.

31. Edmund S. Glenn, "Across the Cultural Barrier," in *The Key Reporter,* 31.1 (Autumn 1965), p. 8.

32. Fung (Feng) Yu-lan, *Hsin Shih Lun* (Changsha: Commercial Press, 1940), pp. 66–67. Few Western language works on hsiang-ch'i are available. Karl Gruber, *Das chinesische Schachspiel; Einführung mit Aufgaben und Partien* (Peking: Siebenberg-Verlag, 1937) is recommended. The translation in the text is free.

APPENDIX I

1. The reader may wonder whether it is valid to base generalizations as to Chinese behavior on the predominantly Japanese source material available. Careful evaluation of the data so gleaned will indeed be necessary before hasty application to the Chinese case is possible. Probably the relatively few Chinese sources will prove more relevant than the plethora of Japanese ones.

2. Kensaku Segoe (ed.), *Meiji gofu* (Tokyo: Nihon Keizai Shimbunsha, 1959), bibliography, pp. 873–989.

3. See *Free China Weekly,* August 21, 1966, p. 2; feature article on wei-ch'i with several references to its military foundations. As more scholarly studies we may note H. Remus, "Simulation of a Learning Machine for Playing Go," *Proc. IFIP Congress 62, Munich* (Amsterdam: North Holland Publishing Company, 1962), pp. 192–94; E. Thorp and W. Walden, "A Partial Analysis of Go," *The (British)*

Computer Journal, 7.3 (1964), pp. 203–207; I. J. Good, "The Mystery of Go," *New Scientist*, No. 427 (January 21, 1965), pp. 172–74; and E. Thorp and W. Walden, "A Computer-assisted Study of Go on mxn Boards," unpublished. I am indebted to Professor John M. H. Olmsted for calling this last work to my attention.

4. Reprinted in Simon, *Models of Man*, pp. 241–60. We should also note, in passing, work on computerizing go-moku strategy in E. Dale and E. Michie (eds.), *Machine Intelligence: 2* (Edinburgh: Oliver and Boyd, 1968). Go-moku is a game of strategy played with wei-ch'i pieces on a wei-ch'i board but with different objectives from those of wei-ch'i.

5. In Smith, *The Game of Go*, pp. 103–10.

6. In particular, studies conducted in the gaming section of the *Journal of Conflict Resolution*. See, for example, Stuart Oskamp and Daniel Perlman, "Factors Affecting Cooperation in a Prisoner's Dilemma Game," JCR, 9.3 (September 1965), 359–74 and bibliography.

7. Compare with a similar list in Michael Elliott-Bateman, *Defeat in the East* (London: Oxford University Press, 1967), p. 73. Refer also to Ralph K. White, "Misperception and the Vietnam War," *The Journal of Social Issues*, 22.3 (July 1966), pp. 1–164.

INDEX

See also Appendix III: Glossary of Wei-ch'i and Analogic Wei-ch'i Terms.